FOLKLORE OF THE TELUGUS

FOLKLORE OF THE TELUGUS

A COLLECTION OF FORTY-TWO HIGHLY AMUSING AND INSTRUCTIVE TALES

BY

G. R. SUBRAMIAH, PANTULU

GYAN

Published by

GYAN

Gyan Publishing House
5, Ansari Road
Daryaganj, New Delhi-110002
Phone: 011-47034999, 9811692060
E-mail: books@gyanbooks.com

Distribution Network
gyanbooks.com
India, USA, Canada, UK, Australia, France

ISBN : 978-81-212-3393-4 (PB)
First Published, 1905

2nd Impression 2020

Printed at: Gyan Press, Delhi.

Folklore of the Telugus
Author: G. R. Subramiah, Pantulu

Folk-lore of the Telugus.

A COLLECTION OF FORTY-TWO HIGHLY AMUSING AND INSTRUCTIVE TALES.

BY

G. R. SUBRAMIAH PANTULU.

PRICE ANNAS EIGHT.
To subscribers of the "Indian Review," Annas Four.

PUBLISHED BY

G. A. NATESAN & CO., ESPLANADE,
Madras.

NOTE.

These Tales appeared in the pages of the "Indian Antiquary" some years ago at various intervals. For the first time they are now published in book form.

CONTENTS.

INTRODUCTION.

——:o:——

IT is within every person's experience to enjoy with all attention the tales told by his grand old dames, to climb their knees, to share the envied kiss. There is hardly anybody, I think, who does not look back with fond attachment to those home associations, with those innocent sweet simple pleasures, whence first we started into life's long race. We feel them, while the wings of fancy still are free, even in age and at our latest day. While the unthinking mind is satisfied with these grandmothers' tales as such, the thinking mind goes a step further and endeavours to gather knowledge from these tales of childhood. There are a good many to whom familiarity breeds contempt, and who, in blissful ignorance, scoff at folklore. But the ethnologist cannot fail to regard it as a *sine qua non* of the study of the racial development. There are many in whom grandeur hears with a disdainful smile these short and simple annals of the poor. But it ought not to be forgotten that these cottages of the poor turn out to be the very nurseries of the wisdom and knowledge which the world has accumulated.

Bare facts of history are not sufficient for the serious ethnologist. There are limits to the historian's survey of the world. "Thus far shalt thou go and no further" can be applied to history as to other departments of knowledge as well. When, therefore, history tries to disdain the limits of its little reign, it calls in the assistance of folklore, archæology, phrenology, etc., etc. Though folklore appears to be a very much neglected branch of science, it takes the place of history during the times when there are no records, by throwing a world of light on the manners, customs and religious and social condition of the people whose folklore it is. We all know that every good is not without alloy, and that this visible Nature and this common world is so created that the two things —evil and good—co-exist. We cannot get any knowledge in a concentrated form. If this be something like a universal law of our present condition, if knowledge, for example, cannot be obtained except by hard and often painful application, if health can be secured only by those who are content to pay the price of steady exercise and strict temperance for it, we need not be surprised if the folklorean study is by no means a purely easy affair, one that can be learnt at first sight. Indian folklore presents very often a thick net-work of the natural and the supernatural which exerts a peculiar talismanic influence on the listener. This blending of the natural and the supernatural has taken possession of the Telugu mind to a very great extent, so much so that the ordinary Telugu person fully believes that there can be no gloomier form of infidelity than that which questions the moral attributes of that Great Being in Whose hands lie the final destinies of us all. His ideas of God's dealings with man are so peculiar to himself that none but those intimately acquainted with him can rightly understand them.

FOLK-LORE OF THE TELUGUS.

I.

AN UNSEASONABLE ADVICE.

In the country of Kandahar,* a certain king, Mahavira by name, at a great expense, caused a tank to be dug, two palm-trees deep and a *yôjana* wide, and constructed a bank around it. But all the water in it dried up, notwithstanding a heavy rainfall. The king, seeing that no water remained in the tank he had constructed at so great an expense, was sitting on the bank with a grieved heart, when one Erunda Muni passed that way. The king immediately rose, went and prostrated himself before the sage, seated him, and began to converse with him; when the sage, looking at the sorrowful countenance of the king, asked him the reason for it. To which the king replied:—

"Sir, I had this tank dug at an enormous expense, but not a drop of water remains in it, and this is why I am feeling grieved."

---

* This name in folk-tales, I think, represents always some part of Rajputana.—(Ed. *Ind. Ant.*)

The sage replied :—"Why weep for this? If you mix boiled rice with the blood of a courageous and liberal king, or with the blood from the throat of a revered *yogi* endowed with all virtuous qualities, and offer it to Durga, whose temple is very near the tank, I dare to say that the water will never dry, and that the tank will be as full as the ocean."

The king heard these words and thought of the difficulty of getting a king answering the description. Then he thought that the sage himself answered the purpose excellently well, being endowed with all the necessary qualities. So he drew his sword, cut the sage's throat, mingled his blood with boiled rice and made the necessary offering to Durga. From that day forward, the rain stopped in the tank and it was full to the brim.

Those, therefore, who tender advice to kings must do so in season, for otherwise they will assuredly come to grief.

II.

THE KING AND THE WRESTLER.

While King Nandana was wielding sway over Malabar a wrestler approached him and said that he had toiled hard and learnt the art of fencing and other similar arts, could fight with wild animals, and could even walk with a huge mountain on his head. But he had found no one, except the king, who could give him the wages due to his powers. He had come, therefore, to the king's presence to re-present his grievances and earn a proper livelihood. The king heard him and thought that such a warrior would be serviceable to him, and engaged his services at a hundred pagodas a month.

There was a huge mountain near the city infested with wild beasts which were causing great havoc among the people. The king, therefore, sent for the wrestler and said:—"You declared, you know, that you could carry a mountain on your shoulders. A mountain there is in the neighbourhood, which is the cause of much suffering to the people. Take it away to a distant spot and return hither."

The wrestler promised obedience and on the next day at dawn, the king took him with his ministers, priest, and a retinue of soldiers to the vicinity of the mountain. The wrestler girded up his waistband, tied his turban and stood ready. The king saw him and asked him why he hesitated, and called upon him to take the mountain on his head and go.

The wrestler replied :—"Sir, I humbly gave you to understand that I could carry the mountain on my head, but I did not say that I could lift it up. Kindly command your soldiers, therefore, to tear the mountain up and place it on my head, and I will then carry it to whatever place you may command me."

III.

THE OLD WOMAN, THE COCK AND THE CHAFING DISH.

In the village of Pennagarai, on the road from Conjeeveram to Wandiwash, there lived an old woman who had a chafing dish and a cock. Day after day at early morn, when the first streaks of light were visible, the cock would crow. All the villagers would then rise, procure fire at her house and go their ways. This state of affairs had run on for a long time, till the old dame took into her head that the day dawned because her cock crew. She observed that all the villagers cooked and ate after getting fire from her house, and she wanted to see how the day could dawn if she quitted the village, and how the villagers would manage to eat. So she went, unknown to anybody in the village, to a wood afar off with her cock and her chafing dish and sat down there. The next morrow, all the villagers arose, came as usual to the old woman's house, but not finding her there, thought she must have gone somewhere on some errand, fetched fire from some other quarter and performed each his respective duty. In the meantime the old woman fasted in the wood until dusk, when a villager passed by to some other place on a particular errand. She called to him and said:—"I was not in the village this morning, has it dawned there? Have the people procured fire? Have they all eaten?"

He laughed and said:—"Do you think that the whole world depends entirely on your cock and your dish? Why do you sit fasting here? Get up and go home."

She heard him and was abashed, and renouncing the foolish vanity which had made her think that all the world existed through her, she lived happily.

IV.

THE DEAF FRIEND.

In a certain village there lived a merchant who had a deaf friend. The latter learning that the former was ill, went to enquire after him, and while going along the road, determined to hold the following conversation with his sick friend; "After the usual greeting, I will first ask, 'well, Sir, how do you feel yourself to-day'? He will reply, 'better,' and I shall rejoin, 'very good.' I will then make enquiries about his diet, and he will reply 'rice without salt,' and I shall rejoin, 'may it do you much service.' I shall then put the question, 'pray, who is your doctor'? He will, of course, tell me that such and such a person is his doctor and I may safely add, may God assist him in the fulfilment of his work.'"

At length, having come to a resolve, he reached the house, and after the usual greetings seated himself near the patient and said:—

"My friend, how are you"?

To which the patient replied :—" I am very much troubled with a virulent attack of fever."

The deaf man, not understanding what he said, thought that he was answering according to the plan he had settled beforehand, and responded :—" Very good : I hope God will keep you so !"

The patient, who was already peevish with the disease, was made more so by this speech of his deaf companion. The latter next asked what his diet was. and was told that it was the dust of the earth !

" May it do you much good," said he ! "and pray, my good friend, which doctor attends you " ?

The sick merchant, boiling with wrath cried :—" Doctor ? Death himself."

" Very well. may God speed his medicines !" said the deaf companion, and returned home.

V

THE SAGACIOUS MINISTER.

Sultan Mahmud* used to wage war on foreign countries and to oppress his people at home. His whole dominions lay consequently desolate. Upon this his minister thought that it was imperative to contrive some stratagem by which the king would turn out a good ruler. Accordingly, whenever he spoke to the king he used to relate how he had once been a pupil of a certain *Sannyasin* and had learnt the language of birds.

One day, as the king and the minister were returning from the hunt, two owls were sitting screaming upon a tree by the road-side. The king, hearing the noises, called upon his minister to tell him what the birds were conversing about. The premier listened for a short time, as though he really understood the conversation, and then

---

* (There have been so many Mahamud Śhahs in the Dakhan that it is difficult to say which of them is meant in this story. The probability is it refers to the very notable doings of the Tughlaks, of whom Sultan Mahmud Tughlak was the last (1394-1413 A.D.) —Ed., *Ind. Ant.*)

told the king that they were not words fit for him to hear. The king, however, insisted upon hearing the words.

The vizier, therefore, represented the conversation to be as follows:—"One of the owls had a son and the other a daughter, and the two parent-birds are negotiating a marriage between their children. The former parent said to the latter:— 'Then, you will give your daughter to my son, but will you give him fifty ruined villages'? To which the latter parent replied:— 'While our Sultân Mahmûd by the grace of the Almighty rules so happily, can there be a dearth of ruined villages? You only asked me for a paltry fifty, I will give you five hundred."

When the Sultân heard this, he was very much grieved at heart. So he at once ordered the rebuilding of all the ruined villages in the realm, and made his subjects happy and prosperous.

VI.

THE LION AND THE JACKAL.

In the Dandaka forest was a lion which was in the habit of attacking and consuming all the beasts thereof. To rid themselves from the constant fear in which they were kept on his approach, all the other animals proposed to supply the lion with an animal a day if it would not attack them any longer. This promise was agreed to, and kept up for some time. Some time after, it fell to the lot of a fox to be sent to the lion, who, by no means relishing the idea of being devoured, walked slowly along, thinking all the while of some plan by which to put an end to the lion and save his own life. The lion, not finding the animal at the proper moment, was very much enraged, and insisted upon an explanation of the delay. The fox rejoined:—"Sir, another fox was sent under my charge by all the animals of the forest as an offering for you, but on the road I met another lion, who took away your meal, and told me to tell you of it."

The lion ordered the fox to take him instantly to the place of his enemy. The cunning fox took the lion to the side of a well, and, saying that the other lion was in it, begged the lion to take him in his arms that he might also have a peep into the well. When the lion saw the reflection of himself in the waters with the fox in his arms, he instantly came to the conclusion that he was looking on his enemy; and having let the fox drop, made a furious leap into the well and immediately perished.

VII

DREAM CONSCIOUSNESS.

There was a harlot in the city of Kalyanapura, who was in the habit of fleecing a hundred pagodas from whomsoever might appear to her in her dreams. It came to pass that on a certain night a Brahman appeared to her in a dream. She described him to her servants, and told them to fetch him and extort the money from him. They seized the Brahman as he was going along the road, and told him of the affair, and demanded the money. The Brahman was very much troubled, and pleaded poverty, but they would not let him go under any circumstances. He accordingly represented his grievances to the king who sent for the woman and demanded an explanation of her procedure.

She replied that she demanded the money as the Brahman appeared to her in her dream. The king said that he would pay her the amount if she should wait a little. He accordingly caused a post to be fixed in the street and the sum tied to the hem of a garment and suspended from the top of the pole. He then placed a mirror underneath, and sent for the woman, and told her what he had done and called upon her to put her hand into the mirror and receive the money. She informed him of the impossibility of taking the money by putting her hand into the mirror, and requested the king to order somebody to climb up the post and bring the money down. But the king replied :—"As the Brahman appeared to you only in a dream, you may take the money that appears in a mirror ; I cannot order anybody to hand you over the bundle."

On hearing this, the harlot felt quite abashed, bent down her head and went away. It is, therefore, necessary that those who settle disputes should be conversant with tricks.

VIII.

THE INEVITABILITY OF THE LAW OF KARMA.

There was a weaver in the Karnataka, Haimantaka by name, who wove both coarse cloth and fine linen. But as his profits in the calling were very meagre, he was not able to make both ends meet. Adjacent to his abode was another of the same profession, Dhimanta who lived happily on the large income he derived by weaving coarse rough fabric. Once upon a time Haimantaka approached his wife and represented his grievances to her, told her how, despite his intelligence in his art, he was not able to eke out a livelihood, and how much better placed his brother-weaver was, though weaving only a coarse stuff.

"My talents are unknown to any one in the place," said he, and determined to quit his home for another place with the object of amassing as much wealth as possible.

His wife rejoined :—"Of what avail is your going to a distant quarter? You will get only as much as it has fallen to your lot to earn."

Despite her remonstrances, he quit his bode, went and settled for a time in a far-off ountry, wove such clothes as were in consonnce with the requirements of the place, made onsiderable money by the transaction, and /ended his way home. On the way he stayed t an inn, and securing his treasure in a corner /ent to rest for the night. While he was enoying 'the honey heavy dew' of slumber, hieves rushed into the inn and purloined very item of property, so that when he ose up the next morning he found to is utter disappointment and distress that he ad nothing left. He thus learnt, very dearly, ndeed, the truth of his wife's statements, from he school of experience. And, feeling very lespondent, lived upon such small gains as he ould make at home. The moral of this is: nlucky anywhere, unlucky everywhere!

IX.

THE WASHERMAN MINISTER.

The King of Kalinga had a washerman who used to wash his cloths exceedingly well and bring and give them to him daily. One day, the king was exceedingly pleased with the scrupulously clean manner in which the clothes were brought to him and promised the washerman to grant any one prayer he might make. The washerman looked at the king and said that he was most anxious to become the king's minister, and requested the king to bestow the post on him. The king did so, dispensing with the services of his old minister, who had served him for a very long time.

It came to pass that, not long afterwards, a certain other king having heard of the weakness of the washerman minister, raised a huge army and gave battle. His master having heard of what had come to pass, called upon the new minister to muster his forces, to which he replied that as he had already made the necessary preparations, there was no cause to fear the enemy. The king fully believed in this statement, but was sorely disappointed, for not long afterwards the city was bombarded by the hostile armies. The king sent at once to the minister, told him of what had happened and enquired of him as to the arrangements he had made.

The minister responded:—"There is nothing to fear in what has come to pass. But I find that the task of ruling a kingdom is a big affair, and while I was thinking of how best to rid ourselves of this difficulty, the enemy chanced to enter and blockade the city. Let them, therefore, undergo the perils of governing the kingdom. As for me, I used to wash the cloths of about a hundred families in this city but since my elevation to the ministership I have had to give up my calling. I will now, therefore, resume it, and give you one-half the work and reserve the other half for myself; the calling being no trouble to me. On these considerations I have made no preparations for war."

The king was very much grieved when he heard this, but thought the result to be the natural punishment of linking himself to a fool.

staggered, but considering that he was not likely to cheat his brother entrusted the whole sum to him. He took it and quietly went away to a far off place.

Then the elder brother, not finding the younger one, returned overwhelmed with sorrow to his own abode, went to the old woman, and said that he did not know what had become of his brother. He, therefore, called upon her to return the whole of the sum entrusted to her. The old woman told him what had happened a few days before; how his younger brother misrepresented the state of affairs, and had walked away with the whole amount.

On hearing this, he began to dispute with the old woman, and brought her before a court of justice. The magistrate heard both the plaintiff and the defendant in the suit in full, saw how the old woman had been duped, called the man and decided as follows :— " The money was entrusted to the woman on the underrstanding that it should be returned when *both* of you came back and demanded it. It is not fair, therefore, to ask her to pay back the amount when you come and ask for it singly. If you are in need of money, therefore, fetch out your brother."

The man was unable to answer this argument and went his own way.

XI.

DURBUDDHI AND SUBUDDHI.

At Avanti lived two merchants, Durbuddhi and Subuddhi by name. These two men went to a foreign country, amassed much wealth there, and returned, and buried unknown to anybody the whole of their riches under a huge tamarind tree very near the town and went to their respective houses.

Not long after, Durbuddhi went clandestinely to the spot, purloined the whole treasure and carried it away to his house. A few days after the incident, both of them conjointly went to the tree and found to their sad disappointment that the treasure was gone. Upon this Durbuddhi accused the other of having secreted the treasure, dragged him before a court of justice, and carried a complaint against him, saying that Subuddhi alone had carried off, unknown to him, the treasure which they jointly buried under the tree, and requested that justice be done in the case.

The judge looked at him, and called upon him to prove the truth of his accusation against Subuddhi. Durbuddhi said that he would prove it by the tree itself under which the treasure was buried. The judge replied that he would investigate the affair the next day.

Meanwhile, Durbuddhi took his father along with him, placed him in the hollow of the tree, and instructed him to answer favourably (to himself) the judge's queries on the morrow. The next day, the judge, according to promise, came with his attendants near the tree and asked who had taken away the money. To the intense astonishment of the by-standers (the man inside) the tree accused Subuddhi of having secreted the money. But the judge was not a man to give in so easily. After a little reflection he caused some straw to be brought, stuffed the hollow with it, and set fire to it. The man inside was suffocated and fell out of the tree dead. The judge, perceiving the deceit that Durbuddhi had played, came to the conclusion that it was he who had walked away with the money. He caused, therefore, all the money to be brought and given over to Subuddhi.

Durbuddhi having paid very dearly for the deceit he had played—in the loss of his riches and his father to boot—went home with a very sad heart.

XII.

CONCENTRATION

At Vizagapatam lived two friends, one of whom used to perform with care the morning ablutions at dawn, and proceeding to the temple remained there for a long time circumambulating the deity. The other was a frequenter of brothels, and passed his time in frivolous conversation with prostitutes. The former though a frequenter of the temple, always had his heart with his friend who led so evil a life and was overwhelmed with grief that he did not follow in his friend's footsteps. The latter was, however, ashamed of his depraved character and was extremely sorry that he did not follow the virtuous ways of his friend.

This went on for a time, and then they both breathed their last. But the former went to Hell, and the latter to Heaven. The sage Narada, seeing the fate of these two, approached the Almighty and said :—" O God! Hell has fallen to the lot of the man who spent his days in your temple, while you have given Heaven and final beatitude to the fellow who never for a moment thought of you, and delighted always in the conversation of women of ill-fame. If you, who are all-powerful, perpetrate such barefaced injustice, who in the world will adore you"?

The Almighty smiled on hearing these words and said that he gave the latter man redemption, for, though a frequenter of houses of ill-fame, he centred his mind on the deity; while the other who frequented the temple diverted his attention to other matters and totally forgot the deity. Hell, therefore, had become his lot. Thus we see that upon the purity of the mind depends the good or evil state we attain after death.

XIII.

Dwijakirtti, King of Cholamandaḷa, had three sons. As he was old and no longer capable of guiding the helm of the State, he resolved to give his kingdom over to any of his sons who might be fit to rule.

In order, therefore, to ascertain their respective capabilities, he sent for his eldest son first and asked him what he most desired. He replied that he was most anxious to have around him the best logicians, grammarians, rhetoricians, and other men of science, and to pass his time in the study of the *Rámáyana*, *Mahábhárata*, and other sacred books. The king thereupon gave him a few villages for his upkeep, and told him to go and do according to his wishes.

He then sent for his second son and asked him what he desired most. He replied, "I am anxious to acquire much wealth, and visit sacred shrines." The king thereupon gave him the money necessary, and sent him on his pilgrimage.

He then sent for the third son and asked him what his desire was. He replied, "to acquire a kingdom, levy a great army, protect the people, make the provinces fruitful, and thus acquire a good reputation."

The king was much gratified at these words, and thinking that he was the fittest person to rule the kingdom, made over charge of the kingdom to him. The son assumed the reins of government, treated his people with justice and generosity, and consequently his people flourished.

You should, therefore, enquire into the capabilities of the person, and his mental tendencies, before entrusting him with authority.

XIV.

THE WASHERMAN OF BENARES.

At Benares lived a washerman, who had an ass and a dog. One night some burglars made a chink in the wall, and waited till he should go to bed to break in and rob all his property. The dog was then absent from the spot; but the ass, seeing the robbers enter the master's house, divined what would happen, and how the house would be rid of all its valuables in no time, and thought that, if the dog were here, he would bark loudly, awake the master, and prevent the household property from being robbed. But he did not know when the dog would come; and thought that nobody ought to be indifferent to his master's affairs, especially in a time of sore distress. He ought, therefore, to bray and thus awake the master—so he brayed to the top of his voice. The washerman hearing the ass bray, and thinking that he was unnecessarily awakened by it, lost his temper, took a stick, beat it well, lay down, and was enjoying sound sleep once again, when the robbers broke in and began plundering the house. At this juncture the dog returned. The ass, seeing the dog, narrated to him what had happened; how the thieves broke into the house and carried off the greater part of the property; how he had brayed, wishing to prevent the occurrence; how it was misunderstood by their master; what a severe drubbing he had received, and so on. He requested the dog at any rate to bark and let the master know the fact. Thereupon the dog began to bark loudly. The washerman hearing it and thinking that the house was being broken open by robbers, rose immediately and searching into every corner of the house,found that the thieves had carried everything off, and was very much grieved.

Moral :—Let the shoemaker stick to his last.

XV.

TO ESCAPE SCOT-FREE.

A certain King of the Karnatak had a flower-garden, in which he spent most of his leisure hours. He had a minister, whose son was in the habit of going daily to the garden and purloining the flowers. The king, missing a number of them day after day, told the gardeners in charge to be on the alert to apprehend the rogue and bring him before him. They accordingly kept watch, caught the minister's son red-handed, put him into a conveyance and took him to the king's palace. The minister was at the time standing at the gate. Those who were near him told him what had happened, how his son had stolen the flowers, how he was caught by the gardeners in the very act of stealing, how he was being conveyed before the king, and wanted the minister to save his son from the infamy. The minister thereupon loudly answered, "It is of no consequence, if he has a mouth, he will live." The son, hearing this, quickly perceived the exact import of his father's words, and immediately ate all the flowers. When they brought him before the king, he asked the boy why he had stolen the flowers. To which the boy said that they brought him there unjustly, for he only went to see the garden, but did not steal anything. As there were no flowers found upon him, the king believed this, and having punished the gardeners sent them away.

Thus, a ready person may always get him self out of a scrape.

XVI.

TRUTH WILL COME TO LIGHT.

In days long gone by, there lived a wealthy merchant at Delhi. One of his servants purloined some of the property in the house and absconded the next day. The merchant thereupon instituted every search for the thief, but to no avail. Not long after, the merchant chanced to go to another city for business purposes. He there saw the servant who had committed the robbery walking in the street, so he seized him and taxed him with having stolen the property and absconding; but the fellow seized the merchant by the waist-cloth and clamorously demanded his property, saying that the merchant was his servant, that he had stolen the goods out of his house, that he had been looking out for him for many a day, and had now found him. He wanted him, therefore, to hand over the property and then go about his business. On this the real and the false merchants, still disputing, went before the Magistrate and represented their grievances. The Magistrate reflected a little, and ordered them both to put their heads through a window, and calling the executioner, said to him, "whoever is the servant, cut off his head." Now it came to pass that the fellow who had committed the robbery being really the servant, and hearing that they were going to cut off his head, withdrew it, while the merchant, on the contrary, never removed his head from the window. On this, the Magistrate discerning that the man, who withdrew his head, was really the servant who had robbed the house of the merchant, punished him severely.

XVII.

THE BRAHMAN AND HIS TWO WIVES.

In the Dakhan lived a Brahman who had two wives. To the elder of these a son was born. When the son was about ten months old, the old Brahman set out with his family on a pilgrimage to Benares, but he unfortunately died on his way. The two women thereupon went to an adjacent *agraharam* (the Brahmans' quarters in a city or village), and remained there, rearing the boy with great affection : so much so that the child knew not which of the two was his real mother. But one day the younger lady quarrelled with the elder, and, declaring that she would no longer remain with her, took the child and set out to go home. The elder thereupon seized the child and demanded of the other why she was taking him away. The younger replied that as she had borne the child she was going away with him. So the two still disputing went to the Judge and told their story. He reflected a little, called his servants and ordered them to divide the child in twain and to give each a half. The younger lady remained silent, but the elder, being the real mother, was of opinion that so long as the child did but live it was enough; and, not consenting the Judge's proposal, said to him that the child was not her own, and requested him to give it to the other lady. The Judge, hearing these words, decided that the elder lady was the child's mother, and had the boy given to her.

XVIII.

VANITY OF HUMAN WISHES.

King Jayachchandra had two favourites, one a Mussalman and the other a Brahman, to whom he was constantly giving presents, by means of which they grew rich and lived happily. One day the king asked them by whose favour they enjoyed their happiness. The Mussalman immediately replied that he was indebted for his, solely to the sovereign; but the Brahman declared that he derived his from the grace of the Almighty. The king, wishing to put their assertions to the test, filled a pumpkin with pearls, which he delivered to the Mussalman, and at the same time presented the Brahman with two *fanams*. On their way home the former, not knowing the contents of the pumpkin, began to grumble at the king's present, and told the latter that he would sell it to him for his two *fanams*, to which the Brahman consented. When he broke it and found the immense wealth that it contained, he returned with great glee, and related the adventure to the King, whose vanity was completely cured by this occurrence. Unassisted by the hand of Providence human endeavours are fruitless.

XIX.

THE MUSSALMAN AND THE ROBBER.

There lived at Rajahmundry a Mussalman whose house was robbed one night. After careful search he traced some of the lost articles to the house of a person, whom he suspected for more reasons than one to be the rogue, and took him therefore before the Judge. The Judge asked the Mussalman if he had any positive proof that the prisoner was the person who had robbed his house. He answered in the negative; whereupon the Judge told him that he must dismiss the case, as he was strictly forbidden by the law to enquire into cases, where there were no eye-witnesses to the fact. On hearing this, the Mussalman removed one of his slipppers and began to beat the rogue. The Judge, in a great passion, asked him what the matter was. He told him that it was because he had not communicated to him beforehand his intention of robbing his house, in order that he might have witnesses ready to prove his villany. The Judge was very much troubled at this reply and remained silent.

XX.

THE SWAN AND THE CROW.

A crow perched on a banyan tree near the sea-shore, saw a swan passing by and asked where it was going, to which the latter replied that it was going to the Mânasasaras. The crow thereupon was extremely anxious to accompany the swan, and requested the latter to take it along with it. The swan, hearing these words, said, "O crow, where is the Mânasasaras and where are you? How great is the distance between you and the *saras*?" The crow was very much enraged at the reply, and said, "You speak without knowing what you are about. If you examine the real truth, you will find that I can fly quicker than yourself. I will exemplify this at once—do you set out and come with me?" So saying, it soared up the skies and went a short distance along with the swan. Afterwards it flew ten yards in advance, and again coming back to the swan said jocosely. "Why, you said something about flying quicker than I, and yet you don't accompany me; the fact of the matter is that you, without looking into your own powers, had trifled with me." By the time that the crow had gone a little further, it became tired and unable to fly along and was in sore distress. The swan thereupon laughing placed it on its own wings and prevented it from falling into the waters below, brought it to the shore and left it there.

Thus an impotent fool, who begins by despising the strong and the good, will, in the end, come to degradation.

XXI.

CASTLE-BUILDING.

At Tirupati lived a Brahman in poor circumstances, who received on a certain day a pot of flour as a present from a certain merchant. He took it, and, being very tired, seated himself on the verandah of a house and soliloquized thus, "If I sell this pot of flour, I shall get half a rupee for it, with which I can purchase a kid. This, in a short time, will produce a flock. I will then sell them, and buy cows, buffaloes, etc., and thus in a few years I shall be the master of three thousand head of cattle. I will then purchase a mansion, which I will furnish elegantly, and marry a beautiful damsel who will crown my happiness by giving birth to a son. My wife will be particularly fond of me, but I shall not allow her too much freedom, and shall sometimes send her away with a kick when she comes to caress me." Thus thinking, he thrust out his leg like one really going to kick, struck the pot and broke it into pieces. The flour got mixed with dirt, and all his ideas of happiness vanished.

XXII.

THE PATH TO FAME.

King Jayathratha of Panchala had a son who was gifted with much sense from infancy. One day, beholding the king, he asked him what the sure road to reputation was. The king replied :—" When you rule the kingdom, without oppressing the people, you must find out who are rich and who are poor, and protect the latter by giving them food and clothing from time to time. Thus will you obtain an extended reputation. But, however much you may bestow on the rich, no fame will accrue to you. To give you an example, if rain falls while the crops are withering for want of water, the cloud will obtain fame, but however much it rains in the ocean, no reputation can result to the cloud." Thus speaking and considering how clever the boy was, the king made over half his kingdom to him. The youth assumed the sceptre, confirmed the leases that had been given to the people, and finding out the poor caused food and clothing to be given to them, and cherished them much. He thus obtained great celebrity.

XXIII.

INJUSTICE AS THE RESULT OF IGNORANCE.

At Channapattanam lived an Englishman, who, as he knew no other language than English, kept an interpreter thoroughly conversant with the vernaculars of the country. One day some conjurors came to the gentleman, and, having fixed their bamboo, danced and displayed several feats of agility before him. The gentleman was highly gratified, and sending for his interpreter, told him to give them ten pagodas. The latter took them home, gave them one pagoda and told them to go about their business. As they thought this a poor recompense for their trouble, and suspected that the interpreter had deceived them, they turned to the gentleman, and showing him the pagoda, informed him that his interpreter had given them only this much. As the gentleman was ignorant of their language, he sent for the interpreter and asked him what they were saying. He told him that among the ten pagodas he had given them, they said that that pagoda was a bad one and wanted a better one in exchange for it. The gentleman thereupon became very much enraged and ordered them to be well thrashed and sent away.

They who are ignorant of the vernaculars of the place they inhabit, and believe what others tell them, must necessarily be guilty of injustice.

XXIV.

CHILD IS FATHER OF THE MAN.

A Brâhman well versed in every branch of science, was journeying with his disciples on a pilgrimage to Benâres, and about sun-set one evening, met a young Brâhman boy, who was feeding a herd of cattle near a wood, of whom he asked the distance to the adjacent village, where he proposed to halt for the night. The boy responded :—"Just look at me, at the cattle I am feeding, the forest, and the sun, and your question will be answered; for if the village was not very near, would such a young boy as I am be feeding so many cattle near a forest at this time of the day?" From this sensible response, the Brâhman formed a high opinion of the boy's abilities, and following him home, told his father that the lad was too clever to be employed in feeding cows, and requested that he might be allowed to take him with his other disciples to Benâres, where he would educate him. The father gladly agreed to the proposal, and the lad afterwards turned out a very brilliant character.

XXV.

THE BOY AND THE THIEF.

As a boy was sitting on the brink of a well crying bitterly, a thief came there, and, seeing him, asked him why he was crying. He answered that as he was playing, he looked into that well, when the pearl necklace that was on his neck slipped off and fell into the water. If he should go home without the necklace, his parents would thrash him, and on that account he was crying. The thief, thinking he would be able to steal it, said to him:—"My lad be not afraid, I will go down into the well and get the pearl necklace; do you take care of my clothes?" Having left his clothes on the bank he descended into the well, naked. As soon as he had got to the bottom, the boy took his clothes and ran away with them. The thief, having searched for a long time and not finding the necklace came up again; but not seeing the boy anywhere he exclaimed:—"Even I, who am a rogue, have been deceived by a boy."

Moral:—However clever a person thinks himself, he may be outwitted by others.

XXVI.

INGRATITUDE.

There was a tiger in a certain wood who used to kill and devour all the beasts that inhabited it. One day he caught a wild buffalo, and while eating it, one of its bones stuck in his jaws. Being unable to extract the bone, blood and puss collected there and caused the tiger a good deal of pain. The tiger laid himself down under a tree, and in great pain opened his mouth, and exclaimed thus:—"How shall I extract this? How shall I live? What shall I do?" In this distress he saw a crow upon the tree, and said to him:—"O crow, you see the pain I am suffering from; if you will but extract the bone and restore me to life, I will give you as much as you want from the food I procure every day." The crow was moved by this supplication, and taking compassion on him, entered his mouth from which he took out the bone, and asked the tiger for the flesh he had promised. The tiger replied:—"When you entered my mouth, I did not crush you under my jaws, but allowed you to come out uninjured. Ungrateful for this, do you ask me for flesh? Look to your business."

Thus people in prosperity often forget the friends who have served them in adversity.

XXVII.

KEEP TO YOUR PROMISE.

There lived at Dhârapura a Brâhman, who went one day into the forest to gather some fruits and flowers. At this juncture, a tiger came there, and the Brahman, becoming afraid, tried to make his eacape. The tiger, however, pursued and overtook him. In this sad predicament, the Brahman begged him to spare his life for three days, that he might return home, settle his affairs, and take leave of his family. The tiger asked him what was to be done in the event of his not returning. He replied, there was no fear, for he would take his oath to return. The tiger having consented, he returned home disconsolate, and after employing the three days in settling his affairs and taking leave of his family, he arrived at the prescribed time, at the place where he had appointed to meet the tiger, who was so pleased at his veracity that he allowed him to depart uninjured.

Thus a person who keeps up to his word is always respected.

XXVIII.

PRE-ORDINANCE.

In Jayasthala on the banks of the Kaveri, there lived a Brahman, Durgatha by name. As he was in very indigent circumstances, he used to go a begging to four different villages, come home at about two or three o'clock every day, and cook his own meal and eat. Things went on thus for some time, and when on a certain day the poor Brahman was plodding his weary way homeward, it came to pass that Iswara and his wife were sauntering in the heavens. Parvati, the wife, unable to endure the sight of this poverty-stricken Brahman, took compassion on him, and requested her husband to bless him with riches. Whereupon Iswara replied and said that Brahma had not written on his face that he must enjoy wealth,* and that he must, therefore, live and die a beggar. Parvati thereupon said :—Let me see how this Brahman cannot become wealthy when we will it," and threw a heap of one thousand gold *mohars* on his way. The Brahman came to within ten yards of the heap, when suddenly the thought struck him to see if he could walk like a blind man. He accordingly shut his eyes and passed off the heap of *mohars* on the way.

Moral :—The law of karma (fate) is inevitable.

XXIX.

DUPED BY THE MAJORITY.

There was a Brahman, Vasanthayaji by name, at Sriramapura, on the banks of the Tamraparni. He conceived the idea of performing a *yajna* (sacrifice), and wanted four or five of the best goats for the purpose. He went, therefore, to a neighbouring village, purchased the goats, tied a rope round their necks, and was wending his way home, when four Sudras wanted to appropriate the goats to themselves. One of them, therefore, came and stood before the Brâhman and said, "Why are you carrying a number of mad dogs?" The Brâhman merely thought him a fool who confounded goats with mad dogs. He went on a little further, when another of the Súdras put him the same question, and wanted him to take care, lest the mad dogs should bite him. The Bràhman, on hearing these words, entertained a slight doubt in his mind. While pursuing his track a little further, a third of the Súdras came close by the goats, grew exceedingly angry, and began to rebuke the Bráhman for letting loose a number of mad dogs on the wayfarers. The Brahman, on hearing this, became certain that they must be mad dogs and tried to unloose them, when the last of the Súdras came up and wanted him to tie them up to a tree adjacent, as, by letting them loose, they would fall upon people and bite them. The Bráhman thereupon tied them to a tree and ran away. The Súdras then untied them and took them home.

Moral:—An intelligent person can be duped by a number of men maintaining the same foolish opinion.

XXX.

CHEATS WILL SURELY BE CHEATED.

In the village of Yachavara there lived a Súdra named Isukathakkidigadu (*lit.* the holder of a quantity of sand). One day he wanted to go to another village and started with a *ser* of sand tied to the hem of his garment. At Machavara, an adjacent village, lived another Sudra, Pedathakkidigadu (*lit.* the holder of a quantity of cowdung), who also wanted to go to another village, and started with a viss of cowdung tied to the hem of his garment. They met each other accidentally in the evening, went to the same village, and seated themselves on the *pial* of a rest-house. Isukathakkidi saw the bundle of Pedathakiddi, took it to be a quantity of food, and resolved to reserve it for his own use, and so asked him what it was. Whereupon Pedathakiddi, who entertained the same desires about the bundle of Isukathakkidi, told him that it contained a quantity of food, and asked Isukathakkidi what the contents of his bundle were. To which he replied :—" I have rice with me, but I regret I have not, like you, brought other food with me. I feel exceedingly hungry, but what can I do ?" Pedathakkiddigadu, hearing the pitiful words of his friend, said :—" Do not feel sorry. Let us exchange our bundles. I do not feel hungry just now." They mutually consented to the proposal, exchanged their bundles, and each fearing the other went to a place afar off in different directions, untied their bundles and were extremely amazed.

Moral :— Entertain not thoughts of deceiving others, lest they deceive you.

XXXI.

THE TIGER AND ITS COUNCIL.

At Gannavâra lived a very poor Brâhman, Divasarma, who eked out a livelihood as a beggar. One day, when he chanced to go to the adjacent wood for fuel for his sacrifice, he saw a huge tiger under a spreading banyan tree. Shaking with fear, he bethought him how best he could go home. There were a few lambs near the tiger at the time, who saw the shivering Brâhman and that he had come in innocence of his danger; so they wished to devise means for saving him. The lambs therefore approached the tiger and said:—"O King Tiger your charity knows no bounds. Your fame extends over the four corners of the world. A Brahman has been here for a very long time, eagerly longing to see you." The tiger thereupon was overjoyed and told the lambs to fetch the Brâhman to his presence. Then the lambs went to the Brâhman, told him not to be afraid, and took him along with them to the tiger.

Whereupon the tiger was exceedingly pleased with the Brâhman, and presented him with some of the ornaments of those whom he had slain on previous occasions. The Brahman thereupon was filled with joy, took the jewels home, sold some of them and lived comfortably out of the proceeds of the sale.

Some time after, a neighbouring Brahman, feeling jealous of the former's situation, thought he could also make a fortune by going to the forest, and on going there saw the tiger surrounded by a number of foxes and dogs. These animals, thinking they might share the spoil, reported the coming of the Brahman to the tiger, and had him slain.

Moral:—People will assuredly come to grief if they approach a king when he is surrounded by evil councillors.

XXXII.

A WISE COUNSEL.

In Bengal there was a king who built a huge fort and lived in it with a very large retinue, and was invincible so long as he remained in the fort.

Now, a tributary king (*polygar*) conceived the idea of somehow drawing the king out of his fortress, confining him in prison, and occupying his vast dominions. With this object, he went to the king one day and informed him that on the morrow his son's marriage was to be celebrated, and requested the king to be present on the auspicious occasion. The king consented, but his minister heard the news, approached him, and said :—"You have entertained, I hear, thoughts of going to the Polygar's house. He is a man full of tricks and has large forces. I am sure he will do you some mischief, once you are away from the fort. Do not go to the Polygar."

To which the king replied :—"What care we how full of tricks he is ? He has been so long faithful to us, and, judging him from his antecedents, he will not, we think, do us any harm. Had he entertained such thoughts, why did he not invade our dominions while we remained in the fortress?"

The minister replied :—"As you are invincible, so long as you remain in the fort, he dare not do you any harm. He therefore seeks your friendship. But should you once go out of the fort, you are helpless. He will not suffer the auspicious moment to pass away. He will show you then his spite. To give you an example, the lotus, so long as it remains in water, spreads forth its petals despite the heat of the sun, the sun all the while aiding it. But once it comes out of its proper element (water), the same sun makes it wither away. It is the same with the Polygar and yourself.

The king was exceedingly pleased with these words and refrained from going to the Polygar.

XXXIII.

THE TALISMAN.

At Chatrapur lived four poor friends, who, being in great distress and sorely puzzled how to eke out a livelihood, met at a certain spot to devise means for bettering their condition. They thereupon performed severe austerities to the Káli of the place, who, being pleased with them, appeared to them and asked them what they wanted. They asked her to confer riches and happiness on them. The Goddess thereupon gave each of them a talisman, which was to be carried on the head. They were told to go in a northerly direction, and wherever the talisman fell from the head to dig there, and take whatever came to each person's lot. The four friends set out on their errand, and went a certain distance, when the talisman of the first person fell from his head. When the spot was dug into, an enormous quantity of copper was found. The first man saw the others, and said that he was quite content with his lot, and stopping there, he carried the copper home. After travelling a little more distance, the talisman of the second man fell from his head. The spot was dug into, and an enormous quantity of silver was found. He followed the action of the first friend, and desisted from going any further. The other two travelled for some time longer, when the talisman on the head of one of them fell off. When the spot was dug into, an enormous quantity of gold was found. He, thereupon, told the last friend not to proceed any further, as, with the quantity of gold found, both of them could live happily. But he gave a deaf ear to the advice, and went on for some time longer, till the talisman fell from his head. The spot was dug into, and a quantity of iron was found. He was overcome with grief at his lot, and regretting the neglect of his friend's advice he retraced his steps. But, alas, in this he was sorely disappointed, for he was not able to find his friend. Thereupon immersed in grief he tried to get at the iron that had fallen to his lot, but he was not able to find the iron. Very sorry for his lot, he came back to the town and lived once more by begging.

Moral :—A person who hears not the advice tendered by his most intimate friends will surely come to grief.

XXXIV.

THE CRANE AND THE FISH.

Lake Vimalâvati has been occupied from time immemorial by large numbers of fish. Once upon a time, a crane, which happened to pass by, conceived the idea of preying on them, and stood on the brink of the lake. But it saw the fish going away from it shaking with fear, and so it said:—"I very much regret your going away from me in the belief that birds of my order make you their prey, and that I would do the same. But I have not come here with such an object in view. I, following others of my kind, have killed a good many fish, and became a sinner, but I am now grown very old, and have renounced the world. I am come here to perform penance. Fear not any harm from me. You may roam anywhere you please."

The poor fish believed the wily words of the crane, especially as the crane did not interfere with them at all, though they approached it.

After some time had thus elapsed, the crane appeared to be very much dejected and melancholy. The fish approached it, and asked it what the matter was. To which the crane replied :—"What shall I say? A twelve years' famine will very shortly visit the land. Not a drop of water will then remain in this lake. I am able to know this by second sight, and, as you are my close friends, I cannot resist the temptation of informing you, lest you die when the famine comes."

The fish were exceedingly joyed at the humane nature of the crane, and requested it to save them from the impending peril. The crane, thereupon, informed them, that there was a lake a few yards further off, which would never dry, and that it would be a very happy refuge for the fish. The latter requested the former to take them up and leave them there. The crane, thereupon, took them up one by one and left them in the sun on a mountain-top, and slowly devoured them.

Moral :—We should never, therefore, believe the words of our natural enemies.

XXXV.

THE HARE AND THE ELEPHANTS.

A famine, in days long gone by, once devastated the whole of the southern country, and there was not a drop of water visible in pond, lake, well or tank. The elephants, very much troubled by thirst, went in search of a place where they could satisfy it to their heart's content, and found a tank called Chandrapushkarani. As the tank was full to the brim, they rested there and quenched their thirst, and also found a habitation in the woods adjacent, till the whole country was again green with verdure. But the track of these elephants was full of hares, and they were smashed to pieces under their heavy footsteps. The hares, seeing the calamity that had befallen them, and how they were greatly reduced in numbers, met at a certain spot to devise means for sending the elephants away to a distant spot. One of them said :—Why fear the elephants ? I have devised means to get rid of them."

On a certain moon-light night, it climbed and sat on an adjacent mountain-top, and said to the elephants who came by, as usual, to drink from the tank :—" O, ye elephants, I have been deputed by Chandra (the moon), whose tank it is, to inform you that this tank has been dug under his orders. That is the reason way it goes under the name of Chandra-pushkarani (*lit.*, the moon's tank). He comes here every night and dallies with his wives. For some time past he has been interrupted in his pastime by your advent and meddling with the waters. He is, therefore, very angry with you. Quit the tank instantly, or otherwise, he told me, he would smash you up ere dawn. If you want to see whether he is angry or not, just look into this tank and you will be satisfied."

The elephants were wonder-struck, and seeing the reflection of the moon, agitated by the wind in the waters, mistook it for his wrath with them, bowed to the moon, requested him to excuse them as they had come there in innocence, and desired the hare to intercede with the moon on their behalf. The elephants thereupon, quitted the place instantly, and the hares from that time forward lived comfortably.

———

XXXVI.

AN HONEST SERVANT.

There was a king at Anantapur, Kunthibhoja by name. While he was holding his *darbar*, being seated on his throne, and surrounded by a host of pundits, ministers, and others, a Kshatriya came and bowed and said that he was an expert in archery, and that he came there to serve the king as he was not able to get a living elsewhere. The king engaged his services at one hundred rupees per month. From that day forwards he kept a vigilant watch over the king's palace. On a certain midnight, while the king was sleeping comfortably upstairs, he heard the cries of a woman, called his attendant and asked him what it was. The archer said that he, too, had heard the same cries for ten days past, but, could not say why it was, but that he would make enquiries, should the king command him to do so. The king consented, and followed him *incognito* to see whither he went. He went outside the town, and there saw a woman with dishevelled hair, seated near the temple of Durga, crying at the top of her voice. He asked her who she was and why she was crying. She replied that she was the tutelary Goddess of Kunthibhoja's kingdom, and that as the king was to breathe his last in two or three days more she was crying—for, who would protect her then? The archer then asked her if there were any means by which the king's life could be saved. Whereupon she said that if the archer's son were offered as a sacrifice to Durga, the king would live for a very long time. The archer thereupon consented to the proposal, went home, and informed his son of what had transpired. The son asked him to perform the sacrifice instantly and save the life of the king, for, by the king a good many people lived. The archer then took his son to the temple, drew his sword from the scabbard, and was about to slay him, when Durgä appeared before them, and said that she was so pleased with his bravery that he must desist, and said moreover that she would confer on him any boon he might ask. The archer then requested Durgä to spare the life of king Kunthibhöja, and to bless him with long life and prosperity. Durgä gave him the boon sought for and disappeared. The archer, overcome with joy, sent his son home, and went to the king's palace. The king, who witnessed *incognito* everything that had transpired, quietly reached his palace, went upstairs, and pretended to be asleep. The archer went to the king and said that a woman who had had a quarrel with her husband was weeping bitterly, and that he had pacified her and sent her home. The king feeling grateful to the archer, raised him to the rank of Commander-in-Chief of his forces.

Moral:— Honest servants will not fail to risk their own lives when calamities befall their masters.

XXXVII.

THE THREE FISH.

Three fish lived in the bed of a river. One of these perceived that the water would dry up in the ensuing summer, informed its other companions of the same, and said, further, how they would run the risk of being carried off by the fishermen at the time, and that they should therefore seek a habitation elsewhere. It wanted, therefore, that all of them should go into the current and settle in the sea or in the bed of another river. The other two laughed at the words of their companion. The clever fish, therefore, went and settled in another quarter unaccompanied. Not long after, summer set in, and the waters of the river dried up. A fisherman threw his net into the bed, caught the two fish and put them on the bank. One of them was possessed of some sense and appeared to be dead, remaining motionless, while the other began to jump. The latter therefore was dashed to the ground and smashed to pieces. The former, perceiving the fisherman going away with his net, crawled unperceived and jumped into the waters and lived comfortably.

Moral :—Whoever perceives coming events and tries to avert danger shall surely be happy; and the person who tries to extricate himself from difficulties, even after they happen, may also consider himself lucky, but the man who remains idle will surely come to grief.

XXXVIII.

THE CRANE AND THE SWAN.

In days long gone by there lived on the banks of the Krishnä, a crane on a silk-cotton tree. Once upon a time it beckoned a swan passing by and said:—"Your body resembles mine in colour, but your beak and legs are red. I have not come across a bird of your kind till now. Who are you? What is your errand?"

Whereupon the swan gave the following answer:—"I am a swan, I am an inhabitant of Brahma's Mânasasaras. I am coming thence."

The crane then asked what things were procurable there and what formed the chief article of its food. To which the swan replied:—"As these things are made by angelic hands, it is beyond my comprehension to describe the grandeur of the place; but you may hear some of the important things procurable. In and around that region are found golden earth, ambrosia, gold lotuses, heaps of pearls, clouds of perfumes, and the tree of paradise. Every object thereof is a wonder."

When the swan informed the crane that it partook of the buds of such lotuses, the latter impatiently asked the former if any oysters were procurable there. On receiving a reply in the negative, the latter burst into a fit of laughter and said ;—" Why prattle of the excellences of a place void of oysters ? It is a pity you do not know the excellences of oysters." Thus the crane put the swan to shame.

Moral :—People will talk big about the meanest things if they like them, and disparagingly of the best things if they do not like them.

XXXIX

KING SIBI.

By far the best of monarchs that wielded sway over the Nishâda country was King Sibi, who was the type of virtue, a well-wisher of his subjects. He would even forego his life to protect the refugee. Once upon a time the Gandarvas began praising his talents and virtuous qualities at the Court of their king Dêvêndra, who heard them, and, coming to a resolve to put them to test, assumed the form of a hawk and called upon his friend Agni to take the form of a dove. The hawk, then, pursuing the dove, reached the earth. The dove came to King Sibi and said :—" O King! there comes a hawk to put an end to me, and make me its prey. Shield me." So saying, he took refuge. Not long after, the hawk approached the king and said :—" It is unfair of you to protect my prey, for that will lead to my certain death. Refrain, therefore, from protecting the dove." To which the king replied that he would give the dove's weight of flesh from his body, instead of the dove itself. The hawk consented to the proposal. The king thereupon brought scales, put the dove on one pan and his flesh on the other, and seeing that even a great quantity of his flesh did not equally balance the dove's, the king himself sat in one of the pans, when the scales were rendered equal. Whereupon the hawk and the dove thought very highly of the king, assumed their own forms, stood before the king, praised him, conferred certain boons on him and went to their respective worlds.

Moral:—Good men will even forego their lives in order to protect those who trust in them.

XL.

THE KING AND THE GIANT.

Nârada, the greatest of Rishis, was once upon a time, while on a visit to Nandikêsvara, requested by him to narrate any important news he had of the *lokas* (worlds), whereupon he informed him of the stories told by the two and thirty images on the throne of Vikramarka.

In Vêdanârâyanapura Agrâhâra there lived a Brâhman, Vishnusarma by name who had four sons, Yajnanârâyana, Vêdanârâyana, Vîranârâyana, and Chandrasarma. The first three were thoroughly conversant with Vedic literature and all the *sastras*, and displayed their learning at the courts of various kings, receiving very valuable presents; while the fourth, as he was not instructed in any of the sciences, acted as their servant. Matters went on thus for some time, till the fourth son became disgusted with his lot and resolving to visit foreign parts for the purpose of becoming educated, left his home at dead of night without telling anyone. The next evening he reached the bank of a river near an *agrahara*, performed his daily ablutions in it, and came out to perform the *japa* alone.

A Brahmarâkshasa, dwelling in an adjacent *pipal*-tree, assumed the form of a Brahman, descended from the tree and stood before Chandrasarma, and enquired who he was; whereupon Chandrasarma, thinking him to be a Brâhman of the adjacent *agrahara*, told him his errand and his story. The Brahmarâkshasa then said :—" Well then, you are intent upon learning." Chandrasarma, right glad of the turn events had taken, consented to receive instruction from the supposed Brâhman, who, thereupon, appeared to him in his true colours and asked him not to be afraid of him. But for all that Sarma shook with fear, and shut his eyes, and so the Brahmarâkshasa immediately resumed the form of a Brahman, consoled Chandrasarma, took him up to the top of the *pipal*-tree, taught him without a moment's stop,—without sleep or food for six months,—and then informed him that he was rid of his curse. He himself would now go on a visit to Benâres, but Sarma was at perfect liberty to go home, being completely trained in all the sciences, and ere long would rise to a very prominent position, and he further blessed him with four very intelligent sons. Chandrasarma, thereupon, enquired of his perceptor the circumstances under which he became a Brahmarâkshasa, and why he had to go on a visit to Benâres. To which the latter replied :—" I was living some time ago at Sarâsvatipura, on the banks of the Krishnâ, and learnt the various sciences. While there, a Brâhman pupil visited the place and requested me to instruct him in some of the sciences, which I refused to do, feeling very proud of my learning, and so my would-be pupil became very much infuriated and said :—' Reserve your learning to yourself; you need not teach me at all: I shall learn from some other person,' and cursed me to become a Brahmarâkshasa. Quaking with fear, I requested him to inform me how best I could be relieved of the curse. And he replied :—' After some time, Chandrasarma, a

Brâhman, intent upon learning, will visit foreign parts. You will accidentally meet him on the bank of a river. He will learn the various sciences from you, and if you will then visit Benâres and bathe in the sacred waters of the Ganges, you will be relieved of your curse and become a Brâhman once more.' I, therefore, became a Brahmarâkshasa and took up my abode in yonder *pipal*-tree, eagerly awaiting your arrival. As I have instructed you in all the sciences, I shall now go on a visit to Benâres to rid myself of the curse. Chandrasarma then took a different route, as he had forgotten the way by which he came to *pipal*-tree, and while going through the palace street of Ujâyani, saw the house of a public woman and mistook it for a Brâhman's quarters, and as he was very tired, having had neither sleep nor food for six months past, went in, spread his upper garment on the verandah and quietly went to sleep. Not long after the house-owner's daughter came out, perceived the sleeping person, and thinking that he would be a fit husband for herself went in and informed her mother of the fact with great glee.

The mother, intent upon appropriating the new-comer's money, came out to see if he were a wealthy man, and perceiving him to be a poor Brâhman, became enraged at her daughter. But the daughter gave a deaf ear to her mother's words, and insisted on possessing the Brâhman. The mother consented, as she was unable to win her daughter over to her arguments. The Brâhman did not rise the next morning, nor did he move a muscle. This made the mother inform the king of what had transpired, who immediately sent the palace doctors to the spot. They felt the pulse of the sleeping person, and went and informed the king that as, for some reason or other, he had had neither food nor sleep for six months past, his body should be smeared all over with boiled rice for some time, and if this were repeated for a time, he would enjoy the honey-heavy dew of slumber and would rise. After six months' tending, according to the doctor's advice, Chandrasarma rose one fine morning just as an ordinary person would, who had enjoyed a very refreshing sleep. Then he began to think :—"Whose house is this? Who is this girl? What brought me here? But what care I for all this?" He was preparing to go his own way, when the girl taking hold of the hem of his garment asked him :—"Are you going to quit me? I have been eagerly waiting for you and tending you for these six months. You are my husband: I am your wife." On hearing this, the Bràhman replied:—"I am a Brâhman and you a Sudra, this sort of talk is, therefore, unfair of you. What have I to do with you?" So saying, he rose, but the girl accompanied him closely wheresoever he went. The matter was reported by the townsfolk to the king, who summoned the Brahman and the Sudra girl before him, and as he was not able to effect a compromise between them, he invited a certain number of the best *Pandits* and requested them to judge of the affair, who pacified Chandrasarma by saying that a Brâhman is at liberty to marry from among all the four castes.

The king then married Chandrasarma first

to his *purohit's* daughter, then to his own daughter, thirdly to the daughter of the wealthiest merchants of the localility, and lastly to the girl in question. As the king had no male issue, he transferred one-half of his kingdom with the necessary army to Chandrasarma, retained him at his own place and lived happily. Chandrasarma had four lodgings prepared for his four wives, kept each of them in a separate house, performed his daily ablutions in the house of his Brahman wife, and lived happily, not swerving from the injunctions laid down in the *Sastras*. Some time after the king died and as he had left no sons, Chandrasarma was installed king of the whole realm by the ministers, *purohits*, and the people. He had by his Brâhman wife a son named Vararuchi; by the second, Vikramarka; by the third, Bhatti; and by the fourth, Hari. All the four sons were well educated. Chandrasarma being very much pleased with the noble qualities of Vikramarka, and as he was moreover the collateral grandson of the late monarch, installed him king and made

Bhatti his premier. Vikramarka then prayed to the goddess, Kâli, who, being greatly pleased with his severe austerities, appeared before him and granted him a boon, that he would rule for one thousand years, that neither gods, spirits, demons nor giants should be able to vanquish him, and that he would meet his death by the hand of a child, born to a girl thirteen *months* old. Vikramarka then came home and informed Bhatti of what had transpired, when the latter said that he would extend the period of the life of Vikramarka by an additional one thousand years. On his questioning the former how he was able to grant the boon, Bhatti replied :—"The goddess Kâli has blessed you that you should *rule* for one thousand years. Rule over the kingdom for six months and travel over the world for the other six months, so that by the time you have ruled for one thousand years, you will practically live for two thousands years." Vikramarka was greatly pleased with the tactics of Bhatti and did as directed. He became afterwards one of the world's best rulers.

Once upon a time a *sannyásin* came to Vikramarka, blessed him and gave him a fruit. The same thing was repeated day after day and the king used to give it over to his steward. On a certain day the fruit was given by the king to a monkey standing near, and when the latter bit a portion of it, a large number of diamonds fell out of the fruit. The king was wonderstruck and called upon the steward to produce the fruit entrusted to him. On their being produced and broken open, the king found to his utter amazement an additional number of diamonds. The king, feeling very pleased with the *sannyasin*, enquired of his errand, when the latter informed him that he was intent upon performing a great *tapas*, that he needed therefore the king's help and that he would tell him the business, should he (the king) come to his abode on the fifteenth day from that date at dead of night. He would then help him, for his *tapas* would be fulfilled. The king consented and dressed himself like a warrior, and, with sword in hand, went to the spot appeared respectfully before the *sannyasin* and asked him what he wanted him to do. The *sannyasin* said :—O king ! you do not fail to abide by your promise. I am very glad you have come here. Whenever I intend to perform a *tapas*, one Bethala throws as many obstacles as he can in the way, and never allows it to reach completion. As you are the strongest and bravest of men, if you will bring Bêthàla here, tied hand and foot, there will be no one to throw obstacles in the way of my *tapas*. If you talk to Bêthâla while bringing him here, he will assuredly run away. You should, therefore, not talk to him at all." Vikramarka then enquired the whereabouts of Bêthàla, went and tied him up and carried him on his back. Bêthàla said to him that he would put him a question which if he knowingly failed to answer, would break his head into a thousand pieces :—

"O king ! In days long gone by there lived king named Yasakêthu, who held sway over Sôbhàvatîpura according to the *dharmas* laid own in the *Sastras*. Close to the town was a temple of the goddess Kâlî, to whom the townsfolk were in the habit of performing *jatras* year after year. Once, while the woman of the town were bathing in the temple tank, Dhavala, a washerman of another town, while going to Sobhavatipura on business, passed through the temple and saw the women bathing. He fell in love with one of them, and hid himself in a certain quarter, and not being able to bear the finely-pointed darts of Cupid, followed her to a little distance from her home, promising, meanwhile, to offer the goddess Kâlî his head a few days after the accomplishment of his cherished object. He was terribly love-sick, and did not go to Sôbhâvatîpura at all, but went home and became more and more emaciated day by day. His parents, who learnt the whole affair, enquired of their son of the whereabouts of the girl, went and negotiated with the girl's parents and effected a marriage between the two. A few days after this the girl's parents sent her to her mother-in-law. Some time afterwards, they sent their son to inform the boy's parents and bring his brother-in-law and sister to their house. Dhavala's parents were very glad, and sent their son and daughter-in-law with the new-comer. They set out, and while resting themselves a little on the way near the temple of the goddess Kâlî, Dhavala went in and offered his head as a sacrifice to the goddess, as he had promised, and died. The new-comer, who was eagerly awaiting the arrival of his brother-in-law, not seeing him come out, went into the temple, and to his utter disappointment and sorrow saw his brother-in-law lying there dead, and died himself. The girl, amazed at both her husband and her brother not coming out for so long a time, went into the temple, and was wholly immersed in sorrow and was about to slay herself, when the goddess Kâlî appeared before her and said that she was pleased with her chastity, and that it was unfair of her to venture on suicide, and said further that, if the two heads of the slain be brought and attached to the other parts of the bodies, they would once more come to life. In her haste she brought the head of her husband and attached it to the body of her brother and *vice versa*, and they both rose up. She was now on the horns of a dilemma, and did not know what to do." Bêthâla then asked Vikramarka who should be taken to husband by the girl. Vikramarka replied that as the head is the most essential part of the whole body, to whatsoever body the head of her husband was attached, that man should become her husband. Bêthàla upon this immediately disappeared.

Bêthâla, however, was once more fetched, and he again began to tell a story. "There remained with Sakaṭasringa, King of Mallikâpura, without a moment's severance, his attendant, Kârpataka by name. Once upon a time, the king set out on a hunting excursion with his large army to a wood, mounted a horse, went with Kârpataka to an uninhabited place a great distance off, and being very much fatigued, rested under the leafy spreading branches of a huge *barh* tree, when Kârpataka brought and gave him two fruits of the emblic myrobalan (*amalaka*). The king then went home, and some time after informed Kârpataka that he had conceived a passion for the daughter of the King of Simhaladvîpa (Ceylon), and wanted him to arrange for a marriage between them. Kârpataka set sail in a merchant vessel, which unfortunately was wrecked and all the people perished. Kârpataka alone, while swimming with the greatest difficulty, caught hold of a twig which carried him to Nâgalôkâ, where he saw a temple to Durgâ, at which he rested. He there saw a number of Nâga girls visiting the temple, worshipping the goddess, and dancing and singing. He conceived a passion for one among the number, and communicated it to her maid-servants, who in turn informed the lady. The lady seemed to agree to the proposal and wanted Kârpataka to bathe in a tank near by. No sooner was that done than he found himself, to his utter amazement, floating in the tank of Mallikâpura. He then informed the king of what had transpired. The king, thereupon, wanted Kârpataka to show him the woman. The whole route was retraversed and the woman in the temple to

Durgâ was shewn. The girl with whom Kârpataka had fallen in love, fell in love with the king, and told him that she would supply him with everything, if he should fulfil her cherished object. The king, thereupon, told her that Kârpataka was his son, a fair-looking, intelligent young man, a person who would act up to his promise, cost whatever it might, and that she should marry and live comfortably with him, to which she consented. The king took hold of Kârpataka' s hand, and saying that the union effected between the latter and the Nâga girl was equal to one of the *amalakas* given him, and that he should do some service for the other fruit, went and immersed himself in the waters of the tank, and reached his capital safe. Kârpataka then lived happily with the girl." Bêthâla then asked Vikramarka :— "Which of them did the greatest good ?" To which Vikramarka replied that it is but natural for a servant to do good to his master, but the master repaid him the good, thinking very highly of the servant's services— that must be considered the greatest. Bêthâla on hearing this, once more disappeared.

Bêthâla was again brought, and again began to narrate a story. "In days long gone by there lived at Vijayanagara a king named Danduvakêsa, who married Satyavratâ, and was so wholly immersed in the luxuries of her charms that he was practically dead to the outer world. Tirthadarsi, his minister, was then guiding the helm of the State. It was rumoured abroad, however, that the minister had appropriated the State to himself, and he, not being able to endure the calumny, went away to a foreign place. The king then entrusted his government to another minister of his, and pursued his old habits. After wandering through various countries, Tirthadarsi reached a port, contracted friendship with a merchant there, and remained always with him. One day the merchant informed him that he was about to set sail to an island afar off, and asked him to look after his affairs till he returned. The minister, thereupon, said that he would accompany the merchant, as he could not endure the pangs of separation.

They both went on board the vessel, and saw a very beautiful woman on an island. On being questioned by the minister who she was, the merchant replied that he did not know, but that he saw her every time he crossed that way. As soon as their business was finished, both of them reached home safely. Some time afterwards the minister took leave of the merchant, went to his own place, was received very cordially by the king, who enquired of him why he had left him. To which the minister replied :—'You were wholly immersed in female charms, and as I guided the State, numerous scandals were spread abroad that I had misused my authority, and so I went away to a foreign place. I then made friendship with a merchant, and went on board his vessel to a far off island and there saw near the temple of the goddess Kâlî a large *barh* tree, underneath whose umbrageous branches was a woman, the very type of perfect womanhood.' On hearing this the king was very much astonished, and wanted to see the girl and having received instructions from the minister, reached the island, saw the girl and thought that the minister was an unusually self-controlled man, for every man who had seen her had conceived a passion for her. Thus he praised the minister, and went and prostrated himself before the goddess Kâli, and then approached the girl, who turned her back on him. The king then took hold of the hem of her garment and asked her not to treat him with contempt. The girl, understanding that he was the greatest of kings did according to his wishes. Some time after, the girl went to bathe in the waters of a tank for the observance of a *vrata*, when she was unfortunately devoured by a *rakshasa*. The king, on seeing this, immediately drew his sword and slew the *rakshasa* and drew the girl out of his body. The girl then informed the king why she was devoured by the *rakshasa*, and lived happily with the king as usual. The king then took her to his capital and remained there more than ever addicted to female allurements. The minister then poisoned himself and died." Vikramarka was then questioned by Bêthâla :—Why did the minister die ? For the king's return ? For the king's marrying the girl whom he (the minister) had fallen in love with "? To which Vikramarka replied that the minister poisoned himself because he foolishly communicated to the king the excellence of the girl in question, being fully aware of the king's previous conduct. Bêthâla once more disappeared.

Thus did Bêthâla abscond twenty-four times, and thus was he fetched again and again by Vikramarka.

XLI.

THE GAINING OF FRIENDS.

At Rajahmundry there lived a King Vishnu vardhana by name, who, distressed at the misconduct of his sons, requested a Brahman to instruct them in the paths of virtue. The Brahman, thereupon, began to tell them the following story of the crow, the turtle, the deer and the rat to prove to them the blessings of harmony.

There stood on the banks of the Godavari a huge cotton tree on which birds of the air used to roost at night. Laghupathânaka, king of the crows, woke early one morning and saw a Kirâta fowler who appeared to him a second Yama and said :—" I have seen this man's face at dawn. Some misfortune is sure to happen. It is not wise to remain near him." As he was flying away as quickly as possible, the fowler approached the tree, scattered a little rice, spread his net, and lay in ambush close by. Thereupon Chitragriva, the dove-king, who was flying afar off, saw the rice and said to his fellow-doves :—" Whence cometh this rice in a desert ? We should not crave for this rice. Once upon a time a traveller, through craving a bracelet, was deceived by a tiger and died.

Once upon a time an old tiger bathed and holding sacred grass in its hand stood on the bank of a tank and called aloud to a passer-by to take the golden bracelet which he offered him. The traveller thought to himself :—'This is my luck. Why hesitate ?' So he asked the tiger to show him the bracelet, and the tiger stretched forth his paw and said :—'See, here is the bracelet.' The traveller said:—'You are a cruel beast : how can I trust you' ? The tiger replied :—'True, I was a very cruel beast in my young days, and slew a host of men and cows. As a consequence I lost my wife and children and have to live alone. But a kind man had mercy on me and advised me to give up killing men and cows and practise good actions. I took his advice, and now I am a poor, weak brute. Why can you not trust me ? As you are a poor man I wish to give this in charity to you.

Go and bathe in the tank close by and you can have it.' The greedy fell into the trap, went into the water, and was bogged in the mud. The tiger saw him and said :—'It is a pity you should have fallen into the mire. I will come and pull you out. Be not afraid.' Thus saying he approached him slowly and caught hold of him. The fool as he was dying, cried out :—'This is the result of my stupid covetousness.' "

The moral is that we should do nothing in a hurry.

One of the doves answered :—" What's the good of excessive caution ? If we are to get our food, we must run risks." On this they all flew and were caught in the net.

When they found themselves entangled they turned on their adviser and abused him :— " This is what comes of following your advice." While the other pigeons reproved him Chitra-griva said :—" What is the use of crying over spilt milk ? We are in a mess, and must do our best to get out of it. A thought suggests itself to me. Let us all fly up together and take the net with us. When united even weak creatures can do much." Hearing this, the doves soared up into the sky, saying there cannot be any better suggestion. The fowler amazed thought of catching them when they alighted again, and followed them staring at the sky till they disappeared from his view, when he went home in grief.

When the birds saw this they asked Chitragriva the next thing to be done. He answered:—"I have a friend, the rat-king Hiranayaka, who dwells at Vichithravana on the banks of the Gandak. He can save us by biting the net strings with his strong teeth. Let us go to him." They took his advice and went to Hiranayaka. But the rat hearing the noise of their wings was sore afraid and would not leave his hole. Chitragriva called to him in a loud voice and said:—"Friend why do you not speak to us?" The rat knew his voice and came out at once.

"I am delighted to see my good friend, Chitragriva." When he saw the pigeons caught in the net, he was startled, and said:—"Friend, what is this?" Chitragriva replied :—"Friend, this is the fruit of our destiny." The rat began to gnaw at the threads, but Chitragriva said :—"Friend, this is not the way to do it. First untie the knots of my subjects, and then mine." Hiranayaka replied :—"My teeth are very weak. I cannot cut all the knots. I will try to sever your knots as long as there is strength in my teeth. Then we shall see about the others if I have sufficient strength." To which Chitragriva replied :—"Do as you please. What can we do beyond our strength?" To which Hiranayaka said :—"Have you not heard of the proverb, 'charity begins at home?". Thereupon Chitragriva replied :—"Friend, what you say is true enough. But cannot endure the trouble of my subjects."

Thus pleased Hiranayaka and he set to work and free all the doves, and after entertaining them sent them all home rejoicing.

The *guru* further said :—Hiranayaka then entered his hole. Laghupathanaka, astonished at what he had seen, came and alighted near the hole of Hiranayaka, and said :—"Oh,

Hiranayaka ! I desire your friendship. Have mercy on me and fulfil my desire." Hearing this Hiranayaka from inside the hole, said :— "Who are you ?" To which the crow replied :—" I am a crow. My name is Laghupathânaka.' Hiranayaka laughed at this, and said :—" I am your lawful prey. How can we two be friends ? It will be with us as with the deer who was caught in the trap and owed his life to the crow." "How was that ?" enquired Laghupathânaka. So Hiranayaka went on to say :—

" A deer and a crow once lived in the forest of Mantharavati in the land of Magadha, and were close friends. The deer throve and grew fat until a jackal saw him and thought to himself what a dainty meal he could make of him. So thinking the jackal came to the deer and said :— 'Let us be friends.' 'Who are you ?' asked the deer. 'I am Subuddhi, the jackal, and I desire your friendship.' So the deer took the jackal to his lair and when the crow who was perched on a tree close by saw them he said to the deer :—' Who is your friend' ? 'This is my dear friend, the jackal, Subuddhi,' he answered. To this the crow replied :—' Can you trust a new-comer ? In days of yore, a kite, Jarathgava by name, died through having entertained a cat, which story I shall tell you.

On the banks of the Bhâgirâthi is a large fig tree. In a hole in its trunk there lived Jarathgava, an old kite. The birds that lived on the tree used to share their food with him and thus he managed to live. One day, Thirghakarna, a cat, approached the tree noiselessly, intending to eat the nestlings. They cried out when they saw her, and Jarathgava, hearing the noise, looked out and spied the cat. The cat was sore afraid of the kite, and thought to herself :—' I am in evil case, I can only escape by my cunning.' So the cat stood before the kite and bowed to him, whereupon the kite asked her who she was. 'I am a cat, and people call me Thirghakarna.' To which the kite replied :—' Be off at once, or it will be the worse for you.' To which the kite replied :—' Kindly let me explain.' So the kite enquired the cat's errand. To which she replied :—'I have changed my course of life and become a Brahmachàrin. I have long wished to meet you, and hospitality is a sacred duty.' The kite, in answer, said :—'Cats are very fond of meat, and there are many nestlings here. This is why I spoke.' When the cat heard this, she put her paws to her ears, and invoking the Lord Krishna swore that she had given up animal food, and was now devoted to deeds piety. Hearing these words, the kite requested the cat not to be angry. 'How can a person know the character of a new-comer as soon as he arrives? Come and go as you please.' So the cat became a crony of the kite and used to live in the same hole in the tree.

By and by the cat used to creep out every night and eat some of the nestlings, which when the birds perceived they began to look about. The cat cleared out at once, and the birds found the bones in the nest of the kite and pecked him to pieces.

Therefore it is that I said that we should not trust a new-comer.

Hearing this, the jackal looked indignantly

at the crow, and said :—'You too were a new-comer when you took up with the deer. Is not a castor oil plant considered a huge tree in a treeless plain ? It is only the ignorant that make a difference between a friend and a foe.' Hearing this, the deer said :—'Why all this wrangling ? Let us all spend our days in one place in peace.' On hearing this, the crow consented. The deer, the jackal and the crow lived together in harmony. After some days had passed the jackal said to the deer :—'Friend ! I have seen in the forest a field fully ripe. Accompany me. I will show you the field. So saying the fox took the deer with him and showed him the place. After this the deer began to graze there. The owner of the field noticed it and resolved to kill the beast. So he laid a net at a corner of the field and went home. The animal, as usual, came the next day to the field to graze and was entangled in the meshes and began to think :—'Alas ! I am caught in a net ! What can I do ? Who is there to rescue me ? If my friend the crow chance to come, he might save me.' The jackal was pleased at the sight and thought that his object was gained. So he went up to the deer, who said :—' Friend, come quick and cut the net.' The jackal said :—" This is the holy day of Munîsvara. How can I touch animal sinew on a fast day ? Any other day I am at your service.' Night came on. The crow missing the deer came to look for him and asked him what had happened. ' This comes,' he answered, ' of trusting a false friend.' Meanwhile the farmer came up, aud the crow said :—' He comes like another Yama, and we must act at once. Do as I tell you. Spread out your legs and feign to be dead.' The deer followed his advice, and when the farmer loosed him from the net the crow gave a caw and the deer escaped. Just then the jackal came up in hopes of a meal : but the farmer, vexed at his mishap, killed him with a blow of his cudgel. He that digs a pit for others falls in himself."

When he heard this tale, Laghupathânaka said to Hiranayaka :—" This is foolish talk. Accept me as your friend like Chitragrîva."

To which Hiranayaka replied:—You are fickle-minded. It is not advisable to make an everlasting friendship with the fickle-minded. To add to this, you are my enemy. It is not good to be on terms of intimacy with an enemy, however good he may be. I cannot, therefore, be intimate with you." To which Laghupathanaka replied:—" Why talk so much without understanding my disposition? Hear my last word. I have seen Chitragriva enjoying the pleasure of your company. I desire to be on terms of friendship with you. It is well if you fulfil my prayers. If not, I shall voluntarily starve myself to death and die." Hiranayaka hearing this came out of the hole and said:—" Laghupathânaka, I am very much pleased with you. I shall do what you desire me to do." Thus saying Hiranayaka pleased the crow by his good deeds, let him depart, and entered the hole. From that time forward, the rat and the crow spent their days in friendly intercourse.

Some time after the crow seeing the rat said:—" Comrade, it is very difficult to eke out a livelihood here. I intend, therefore, to quit this desert for a suitable abode." Whereupon Hiranáyaka replied :—"Teeth, hair, nails, and men will not shine if their habitation is gone. The wise person ought, therefore, to give up the idea of quitting a residence." To which the crow replied :—"Friend, your words are weak. Elephants, lions and good men wander wheresoever they will. Crows, birds and cowards perish in their own place, not being able to quit it." Whereupon Hiranyaka said :—"Comrade, where is it that you want to go to?" To which the crow replied :—"We should not quit an old residence without examining a new one. Therefore it is that I have not spoken to you before fixing our new quarters. There is in the forest of Dandaka a tank called Karpuragaura. In it dwells my friend Manthara, the turtle-king. He is a charitable creature. That excellent tortoise will support me with plenty of fish food." Whereupon Hiranayaka said :—"What can I do here after you are gone? Take me, therefore, along with you."

Laghupathanaka hearing this was very much pleased and consented to the proposal. They then began their journey with pleasant conversation on the way and reached the tank in a few days. When Manthara saw them at a distance, he went to meet them, fetched them thither, and feasted them as became their rank.

Laghupathanaka then said to Manthara:—"Comrade, treat this rat-king respectfully. He is the foremost among the virtuous, the ocean of good qualities, and is known as Hiranayaka. Even Sesha is unable to describe his qualities. How much then am I?"

So saying he narrated Hiranayaka's story in detail from the beginning. Manthara then treated Hiranayaka with much respect and said:—"Hiranyaka, what is the cause of your living in a desert?" To which he replied:—

"There was a town named Champakavati which was inhabited by many Sannyasis, among whom was one Chudakarna. He would eat part of the food fetched and would hang the other portion on a wooden peg fixed in the wall and then go to sleep. I would creep noiselessly to it and would every day partake of the food. Once upon a time he was conversing with his friend Vinakarna and was constantly looking up and shaking his rattle and terryfying me. Vinakarna then asked Chudakarna:—'Why is it that you look up and shake your rattle?' To which he replied:—'A rat every day gets up the wooden peg and partakes of the food there. It is a source of very great trouble to me.' Vinakarna hearing this said:—'Where is the rat and where the wooden peg? Where did such little creature get the strength to climb such a great height? There must be some cause for this. Some time ago I went to a Brâhman's house to eat, when the Brâhman called his wife and said:—'To-morrow a few Brâhmans must be fed as it is the new-moon day. What provisions have you collected for it?' To which the housewife replied:—'If the men bring home provisions, the women can cook them. If they do not bring them what can we do?' Whereupon he grew exceedingly angry and turning to his wife said:—'We must manage with the things we possess and not seek what we have not.' To which the housewife agreed and said:—'I shall manage tomorrow's meal with the little that we have.' So saying she washed, pounded and dried a quantity of sesamum. A fowl, then came and scratched away the seed. The Brahman seeing this, said:—'The seasamum seeds have become impure and unfit for a Brahman meal. Go and exchange these for something else and return.' The housewife came the next day into the house to which I was invited to eat, and asked the housewife if she would give ordinary sesamum in exchange for her pounded seed. The housewife gladly agreed to her proposal, took some sesamum seed in a sieve and was conversing when the master asked her what it was that she was bargaining about. To which she said that she received pounded sesamum seed in exchange for a smaller quantity of unhusked seed. The Brahman hearing this, said:—'O fool! would anybody give pounded seed in exchange for unhusked? There must be some reason for her giving it.

Do not cake this grain.' So this rat cannot have such strength and this fixed abode here without a cause.'

While Vinakarna told this tale, Chudakarna heard it, searched and found a hole where the rat was residing. 'Why should it reside here? I shall dig it up.' So saying he took up an axe and dug into my hole and took away all the treasure stored up from many a long day. Being sorely vexed, and unable to earn my daily bread, I was creeping sadly about when Chudakarna one day saw me and said:—" Wealth is the root of all welfare. What is the good of life without money. This rat having lost all his wealth has lost with it his original strength." When the Sannyâsin said this I grew dejected and thought thus within myself:—' It is not right for me to live here any longer. Nor is it proper to communicate my story to others. Chudakarna seeing me not quitting the place aimed a fatal blow at me with his stick which I fortunately escaped. Had it struck me I must have been for long an inhabitant of Yâmalôka. So musing I left the place and came to the jungle where life is easier for us." Manthara hearing this, said :—" Wealth is perishable, and it is useless to hoard it, as you will see from the fate of the miserly jackal."

One day a hunter named Bhairava, of the city of Kalyana Katak, went into the forest. He slew a deer and was carrying it home when he met a wild pig. He aimed an arrow at the beast, which in his death struggle gored him and a great serpent which lay close by. So all three died then and there. Up came the jackal Thirgarava, and seeing the dead bodies rejoiced at the prospect of having abundant food. But in his greediness he thought to himself:—'The meat I will keep for use and meanwhile I will eat the bowstring.' As soon as he began to bite the string the arrow was released and slew him too."

When he heard these words of Manthara he rejoiced and said:—" Now I know the value of a good friend."

One day when they were enjoying themselves in the forest a deer rushed up, pursued by a hunter. The tortoise in his fear shuffled into the water: the rat crept into his hole and the crow flew to the top of a tree. He looked all round, and seeing no sign of danger called to his two friends. They came out and asked the deer what had befallen him. He said:—"My name is Chitranga, and I claim your protection." So they took him into their company, and all four lived pleasantly together.

One day the deer went out alone to graze, and when he did not return at the usual hour they feared lest evil may have befallen him.

They debated which of them should go in search of him. At last the crow said:—"I am the swiftest of birds, and will fly off and learn what has befallen him." He flew and flew high up in the air until he came to the place where the deer had fallen into a snare. The deer delighted to see his friend, said:—"No time must be lost. Hasten and bring the rat Hiranayaka to gnaw the cords of the snare." So the crow went, and placing the rat on his back speedily flew back with him. When the rat succeeded in extricating the deer they asked him how he had fallen into this fresh disaster. "No creature," said he, "can escape his fate. When I was a little fawn one day I fell into a snare, was caught by a hunter and taken to the king's palace. There I was reared as a pet and golden ornaments were hung on my neck. One day when wandering in the city I was chased by boys but the ladies of the royal seraglio found me and tied me up near the chamber of the king. That night a heavy storm of rain came on and I cried out in my joy:—'How delightful is this rain! How sweet the grass will grow for me to eat.' The king wondered to hear a beast talk in the tongue of men, and next day sent for the astrologers and told them what he had heard. They said:—'For a beast to know human speech is an event of ill omen. Your Majesty should perform rites of expiation and send the deer to a distant forest.' So they sent me from that abode of peace and safety and I came to the forest where, as you know, I fell into the snare of the hunter."

Meanwhile the tortoise was anxiously expecting his friends the crow and the rat, and was delighted when they returned after rescuing the deer.

As they were talking the hunter came up and missing the deer from the snare followed his touches. The crow again espied him and warned his friends. The rat got into a hole, the crow flow away and the deer hid himself in a thicket. But the hunter secured the tortoise and was carrying him off when the rat said to the deer:—"You must repay us for rescuing you by saving the tortoise. Go into this pond, and lie down as if you were dead: the crow will sit on your back and seem as about to peck out your eyes. Then the hunter will put down the tortoise and he can escape.

They did as he planned, and the trick succeeded. The tortoise escaped and the four friends were once again united.

XLII.

THE CAT AND THE MOUSE.

There was once a large banyan tree in the midst of an extensive forest, covered with many kinds of creepers, which was the resort of a number of birds and animals. A mouse of great wisdom lived at its foot, having made a hole there with a hundred outlets, and in the branches there lived a cat in great happiness, daily devouring many birds.

Now it happened that a Chandala came into the forest and built a hut for himself, and every evening after sunset he spread his traps, made of leathern strings. Many animals fell into his traps every night, and it so happened that one day the cat, in a moment of heedlessness, was caught.

As soon as his foe the cat was caught, the mouse came out of his hole and began to rove about fearlessly. While trustfully roving through the forest in search of food, the mouse after a little while saw the meat that the Chandala had spread in his trap as a lure. Getting upon the trap the little animal began to eat the flesh, and even got upon his enemy entangled hopelessly in it. Intent upon eating the flesh, he did not mark his own danger, until suddenly he saw another terrible foe in the person of a restless mungoose with fiery eyes, standing on his haunches, with head upraised, licking the corners of his mouth with his tongue. At the same time he beheld yet another foe sitting on a branch of the banyan tree in the shape of a sharp-beaked night-jar.

Encompassed on all sides by danger, and seeing fear in every direction, the mouse, filled with alarm for his safety, made a high resolve. Of his three enemies the cat was in dire distress, and so the mouse, conversant with the science of profit and well acquainted with the occasions on which war should be declared or peace made, gently addressed the cat, saying :—

"I address thee in friendship, O cat! Art thou alive ? I wish thee to live ! I desire the good of us both. O amiable one, thou hast no cause for fear. Thou shalt live in happiness. I will rescue thee, if, indeed, thou dost not slay me. An excellent expedient suggests itself to me, by which thou mayest escape and I obtain great benefit. By reflecting earnestly I have hit upon that expedient for thy sake and for my sake, for it will benefit both of us. There are the mungoose and the owl, both waiting with evil intent. Only so long, O cat, as they do not attack me, is my life safe. Possessed of wisdom as thou art, thou art my friend and I will act towards thee as a friend. Without my help, O cat, thou canst not succeed in tearing the net, but I can cut the net for thee, if thou abstain from killing me. Thou hast lived on this tree and I have lived at its foot. Both of us have dwelt here for many long years. All this is known to thee. He, upon whom nobody places his trust, and he who never trusts another, are never applauded by the wise. Both of them are unhappy. For this reason, let our love for each other increase and let there be union between us. The wise never applaud endeavour when the opportunity for success has passed away. Know that this is the proper time for such an understanding between us. I wish thee to live, and thou also wishest me to live. This our compact also will bring happiness to us both. I will rescue thee and thou wilt also rescue me."

Hearing these well-chosen words, fraught with reason and highly acceptable, the cat spoke in reply :—" I am delighted with thee, O amiable one, blessed be thou that wishest me to live. Do that, without hesitation, which thou thinkest will be of use. I am certainly in great distress. Thou art, if possible, in greater distress still. Let there be a compact between us without delay. If thou rescuest me, thy service shall not go for nothing. I place myself in thy hands. I will wait upon and serve thee like a disciple. I seek thy protection, and will always obey thy behests."

Thus addressed, the mouse, addressing in return the cat who was completely under his control, said these words of grave import and high wisdom :—" Thou hast spoken most magnanimously. It could scarcely be unexpected from one like thee. Listen to me as I disclose my expedient. I will crouch beneath thy body and so shalt thou save me from the owl and the mungoose, and I will cut the noose that entangles thee. I swear by Truth, O friend."

The mouse, having thus made the cat understand his own interest, trustfully crouched beneath his enemy's body. Possessed of learning, and thus assured by the cat, the mouse trustfully laid himself thus under the breast of the cat as if it were the lap of his father or mother. Beholding him thus ensconced the mungoose and the owl both became hopeless of seizing their prey. Indeed, seeing the close intimacy between the mouse and the cat, the owl and the mungoose became alarmed and were filled with wonder, and felt themselves unable to wean the mouse and the cat from their compact. So they both left the spot and went away to their respective abodes.

After this the mouse, conversant with the requirements of time and place, began, as he lay under the body of the cat, to cut the strings of the noose slowly, waiting for a fitting opportunity to finish his work. Distressed by the strings that entangled him, the cat became impatient and said :—" How is it, O amiable one, that thou dost not proceed with haste in thy work? Dost thou disregard me now, having thyself succeeded in thy object? Cut these strings quickly! The hunter will soon be here."

But the mouse, possessed of intelligence, replied with these beneficial words fraught with his own good :—" Wait in silence, O amiable one! Chase all thy fears away. We know the requirements of time. We are not wasting it. When an act is begun at an improper moment, it never becomes profitable when accomplished. If thou art freed at an unseasonable moment, I shall stand in great dread of thee. Do thou, therefore, await the opportunity. When I see the hunter approach the spot armed with weapons, I shall cut the strings at the moment of dire fear to both of us. Freed then, thou wilt ascend the tree. At that time thou wilt not think of anything but thy own life, and it is then that I shall enter my hole in safety."

The cat, who had quickly and properly performed his part of the covenant, now addressed the mouse, who was not expeditious in discharging his:—"I rescued thee from a terrible danger with great promptness, so thou shouldst do what is for my good with greater expedition. If I have ever unconsciously done thee any wrong, thou shouldst not bear this in remembrance. I beg thy forgiveness. Be a little quicker."

But the mouse, possessed of intelligence and wisdom and knowledge of the Scriptures, replied with these excellent words:—"That friendship in which there is fear, and which cannot be kept without fear, should be maintained with great caution, like the hand of the snake charmer at the snake's fangs. He who does not protect himself after having made a covenant with one that is stronger, finds that covenant productive of injury instead of benefit. Nobody is anybody's friend, nobody is anybody's well-wisher; persons become friends or foes only from motives of interest. Interest enlists interest, even as tame elephants help to catch wild individuals of their own species. When a kind act has been accomplished, the doer is scarcely regarded. For this reason, all acts soould be so done that something may remain to be done. So when I set thee free in the presence of the hunter, thou wilt fly for thy life without ever thinking of seizing me. Behold all the strings of this net but one have been cut by me, and I will cut that in time.Be comforted."

While the mouse and the cat were thus talking together, both in serious danger, the night gradually wore away, and a great and terrible fear filled the heart of the cat. When at last morning came, the Chandala appeared on the scene. His visage was frightful. His hair was black and tawny. His lips were very large and his aspect very fierce. A huge mouth extended from ear to ear, and his ears were very long. Armed with weapons and accompanied by a pack of dogs, this grim-looking man appeared on the scene. Beholding one that resembled a messenger of Yama, the cat was penetrated through and through with fright. But the mouse had very quickly cut the remaining string, and the cat ran with speed up the banyan tree. The mouse also quickly fled into his hole. The hunter, who had seen everything, took up the net and quickly left the spot.

Liberated from his great peril, the cat, from the branches of the tree, addressed the mouse:— "I hope thou dost not suspect me of any evil intent. Having given me my life, why dost thou not approach me at a time when friends should enjoy the sweetness of friendship? I have been honored and served by thee to the best of thy power. It behoveth thee now to enjoy the company of my poor self who has become thy friend. Like disciples worshipping their preceptor, all the friends I have, all my relatives and kinsmen, will honour and worship thee. I myself, too, will worship thee. Be thou the lord of my body and home. Be thou the disposer of all my wealth and possessions. Be thou my honored counsellor, and do thou rule me like a father. I swear by my life that thou hast no fear from us."

But the mouse, conversant with all that is productive of the highest good, replied in sweet words that were beneficial to himself:—"Hear how the matter appears to me. Friends should be well examined. Foes also should be well studied. In this world a task like this is regarded by even the learned as a difficult one, depending upon acute intelligence. Friends assume the guise of foes, and foes of friends. When compacts of friendship are formed, it is difficult for either party to understand why the other party is moved. There is no such thing as a foe. There is no such thing in existence as a friend. It is the force of circumstances that creates friends and foes. He who regards his own interests ensured as long as another person lives, and thinks them endangered when another person will cease to live, takes that other person for a friend and considers him such as long as those interests of his are not interfered with. There is no condition that deserves permanently the name either of friendship or hostility. Both arise from considerations of interest and gain. Self-interest is very powerful. He who reposes blind trust in friends, and always behaves with mistrust towards foes without paying any regard to considerations of policy, finds his life unsafe. He who, disregarding all considerations of policy, sets his heart upon an affectionate union with either friends or foes, comes to be regarded as a person whose understanding has been unhinged. One should never repose trust in a person undeserving of trust. Father, mother, son, maternal uncle, sister's son, all are guided by considerations of interest and profit.

"Thou tellest me in sweet words that I am very dear to thee. Hear, however, O friend, the reasons that exist on my side. One becomes dear from an adequate cause. One becomes a foe from an adequate cause. This whole world of creatures is moved by the desire of gain in some form or other. The friendship between two uterine brothers, the love between husband and wife, depends upon interest. I do not know any kind of affection between any persons that does not rest upon some motive of self-interest. One becomes dear for one's liberality, another for his sweet words, a third in consequence of his religious acts. Generally a person becomes dear for the purpose he serves. The affection between us two arose from a sufficient cause. That cause exists no longer. On the other hand, from adequate reason, that affection between us has come to an end. What is that reason, I ask, for which I have become so dear to thee, besides thy desire of making me thy prey? Thou shouldst know that I am not forgetful of this. Time spoils reasons. Thou seekest thy own interests. Others, however, possessed of wisdom, understand theirown interests too.

"Guided, however, by my own interests, I myself am firm in peace and war that are themselves very unstable. The circumstances under which peace is to be made or war declared are changed as quickly as the clouds change their form. This very day thou wert my foe. This very day again thou wert my friend. This very day thou hast once more become my enemy. Behold the levity of the considerations that move living creatures. There was friendship between us as long as there was reason for its existence. That reason, dependent on time, has passed away. Without it, that friendship has also passed away. Thou art by nature my foe. From circumstances thou becamest my friend. That state of things has passed away. The old state of enemity that is natural has come back. Through thy power I was freed from a great danger. Through my power thou hast been freed from a similar danger. Each of us has served the other. There is no need of uniting ourselves again in friendly intercourse. O amiable one, the object thou hadst has been accomplished. The object I had has also been accomplished. Thou hast now no need for me except to make me thy food. I am thy food. Thou art the eater. I am weak. Thou art strong. There cannot be a friendly union between us when we are situated so unequally. I know that thou art hungry. I know that it is thy hour for taking food. Thou art seeking for thy prey, with thy eyes directed towards me. Thou hast sons and wives. Seeing me with thee, would not thy dear spouse and thy loving children cheerfully eat me up?"

Thus soundly rebuked by the mouse, the cat, blushing with shame, addressed the mouse:—

"Truly I swear that to injure a friend is, in my estimation, very censurable. It doth not behove thee, O good friend, to take me for what I am not. I cherish a great friendship for thee in consequence of thy having granted me my life. I am, again, acquainted with the meaning of duty. I am an appreciator of other people's merits. I am very grateful for services received. I am devoted to the service of friends. I am, again, especially devoted to thee. For these reasons, O good friend, it behoveth thee to re-unite thyself with me. O thou that art acquainted with the truths of morality, it behoveth thee not to cherish any suspicion in respect of me."

Then the mouse, reflecting a little, replied with these words of grave import:—"Thou art exceedingly kind. But for all that, I cannot trust thee. I tell thee, O friend, the wise never place themselves, without sufficient reason, in the power of a foe. Having gained his object, the weaker of two parties should not again repose confidence in the stronger. One should never trust a person who does not deserve to be trusted. Nor should one repose blind confidence in one deserving of trust. One should always endeavour to inspire foes with confidence in himself. One should not, however, himself repose confidence in foes. In brief, the highest truth of all in reference to policy is mistrust. For this reason, mistrust of all persons is productive of the greatest good. One like myself should always guard his life from persons like thee. Do thou also protect they life from the Chandala who is now very angry."

While the mouse thus spake, the cat, frightened at the mention of the hunter, hastily leaving the tree ran away with great speed, and the mouse also sought shelter in a hole somewhere else.

The Son-in-law Abroad and other INDIAN FOLK TALES OF FUN, FOLLY, CLEVERNESS, CUNNING, WIT AND HUMOUR. By P. Ramachandra Row, B.A., B.L., Retired Statutory Civilian. Price As. 6. To subscribers of the *Indian Review*, As. 4.

THE VICISSITUDES OF ARYAN CIVILISATION IN INDIA. Being an essay which treats of the history of the Vedic and Buddhistic Polities, explaining their origin, prosperity and decline, by M. M. Kunte, B.A In this book, the strange revolutions through which India has passed during the thousands of years over which her history extends have been reviewed: the principles and conditions of their origin and development have been analysed and the consequences which followed them have been traced with an anxious care which scientific history demands Reduced. **PRICE RS. 1-8.**

LITERARY HISTORY OF INDIA. By R. W. Frazer, LL. B., I.C.S., Lecturer in Telugu and Tamil at University College and the Imperial Institute. With Photogravure Frontispiece. Demy 8vo. cloth. Rs. 10 only.

"This is an excellent, and invaluable book, filling a want which must often have been felt by the reader...The learning and reading which have gone to the compilation of Mr. Frazer's volume are great, yet he handles them with a clearness and order too frequently absent from books of this kind."—*Academy.*

G. A. NATESAN & CO., ESPLANADE, MADRAS.

BOOKS ON

HINDU

Religion, Philosophy, Sociology, Etc.

——:o:——

BHAGAVAD GITA with Sri Sankara's Commentary. By A. Mahadeva Sastri, Cloth, Rs. 4. Board, Rs 3.

LECTURES ON GNANA-YOGA. By Swami Vivekananda. Rs. 2-8.

CONTENTS :—The Song of the Sanyasin ; The Necessity of a universal Religion ; the Real and Apparent Man, Maya and Illusion ; Maya and the Evolution of the Conception of God ; Maya and Freedom ; The Absolute and Manifestation ; Cosmos—Macrocosm and Microcosm Reincarnation, Immortality ; Is the Soul Immortal ; Unity in Diversity ; God in everything ; Realization ; Freedom of the Soul ; Practical Vedanta ; Parts. I, II, III and IV, Vedanta.

LALITA SAHASRANAMA with Bhaskararaya's Commentary. By R. Anantakrishna Sastri. Rs. 3.

VISHNU SAHASRANAMA with Sri Sankara's Commentary. By R. Anantakrishna Sastri. Rs. 1-8.

SIVA SAHASRANAMA STOTRA with Sri Nilakanta's Commentary. By R. Anantakrishna Sastri. Re. 1.

THE HOLY LIVES OF THE AZHWARS OR THE DRAVIDA SAINTS. By A. Govindacharya. Re. 1-8.

THE RATIONALE OF HOLY IMAGE WORSHIP. By A. Govindacharya As. 8.

HINDU RELIGION AND PHILOSOPHY.

SRI BHAGAVAD GITA with Ramanuja's Commentary in English. By A. Govindacharya. Rs. 6.

THE BRAHMA SUTRAS of Sri Madhvacharya, in Sanskrit Devanagiri. By P. Ramachandra Row, *Retired Statutory Civilian.* Re. 1.

FROM COLOMBO TO ALMORA. By Swami Vivekananda. Paper, Rs. 2-8. Cloth, Rs. 3.

THE CHRONOLOGY OF ANCIENT INDIA. By Velandai Gopala Aiyar, B.A., B.L., *Pleader. Chittoor,* FIRST SERIES:—The Beginning of the Kali Yuga; The Date of the Mahabharata War; The Four Yugas. Rs. 1-4.

THE INDIAN WISDOM or Readings from Yoga Visishta: being a collection of 732 wise sayings by N. K. Ramaswami Iyer, B.A., B.L., High Court Vakil, Madras. As. 8.

HINDU THEISM by Sitanath Tattvabhushan. Paper cover. Re. 1.

CONTENTS:— Hindu Theism; Authority and Free-Thought in Religion; the Theosophy of the Upanishads; the Self and its "Sheaths"; Is Nature apparent or real; Incarnation; Re-incarnation; the Ethics of the Upanishads; Bondage and Deliverance; Hindu and Christian Theism compared.

HINDU FEASTS, FASTS AND CEREMONIES—By Pandit S. M. Natesa Sastri, B. A., M. F. L. S. With an introduction by Henry K. Beauchamp, C. I. E., M. R. A. S., F. R. H. S., Editor, *The Madras Mail.* Rs. 1-8.

THE ASHTAVAKRA GITA: a treatise on Advaita Philosophy. Translated into English with brief notes and introduction by Rai Bahadur Lala Baijnath, B. A. As. 8.

HINDU RELIGION AND PHILOSOPHY.

KARMA.— By G. Kasturi Ranga Iyengar, M.A. As. 4.

MINOR UPANISHADS VOL. I comprising Amritabindu and Kaivalya Upanishads with commentaries and Sanskrit Text. As. 10.

KARMA YOGA : a course of eight lectures delivered at New York by Swami Vivekananda. Paper bound. Re. 1.

VEDANTA—THE PHILOSOPHY OF SCIENCE By an Advaitananda. Re. 1.

CONTENTS.–Aum : Advaitism—the Philosophy of Science Vedanta in Brief ; The Philosophy of the Vedanta Sutras ; The Philosophy of the Upanishads ; The Philosophy of the Bhagavad Gita ; Monism, the Philosophy of Science ; The Unknowable ; The Religion of Science ; The Advaitic Table of Being.

THE SRI-BHASHYA OF RAMANUJACHARYA.—Translated into English by Professor M. Ranga Chariar, M.A, and Mr. M. B. Varadaraja Aiyangar, B.A, B.L. Vol. I. with an Analytical outline of contents. Rs. 5.

VEDIC INDIA, (As embodied principally in the Rig-Veda). By Zenaide A. Ragozin, *Member of the Royal Asiatic Society. With Map and Illustrations. Third Edition, Large Crown 8vo., Cloth* Rs. 3-2.

A SHORT ACCOUNT OF THE VEDANTA PHILOSOPHY according to Sankara translated from Dr. Deusen's System of Vedanta by A W. Smart. As 2.

THE TAITTIRIYA UPANISHAD with the commentaries of Sankaracharya, Suresvaracharya and Sayana. Translated by A. Mahadeva Sastriar in 4 parts. In one Vol. Boards, Rs. 4. Cloth, Rs. 5. Available separately.

HINDU RELIGION AND PHILOSOPHY.

THE MYSTICS, ASCETICS AND SAINTS OF INDIA. By John Campbell Oman, *Author of "Indian Life, Religious and Social," etc. Fully illustrated. Medium 8vo., cloth.* Rs. 10-8.

This work is in the main a study of Sadhuism, the name Sadhu being applied in general to Hindu ascetics, monks, or religious mendicants, without reference to their particular sects. It contains also incidentally some account of the faquirs, or ascetics who profess Islam. A great mass of information, which has hitherto been scattered in a number of books are in learned journals difficult of access is here brought within the reach of every one, and many new and interesting facts which have come within the author's personal experience are added, with the result that a tolerably full account has been presented in this volume of the peculiarities of the leading ascetic sects, such as the *Yogis*, *Sannyasis*, *Bairagis*, etc. The question of Indian miracle workers—a subject of perennial interest—is also discussed. In a concluding chapter, the author enters into a comparison of Occidental and Oriental ideals, the latter has especially exemplified by the prevalence of Sadhuism since remote antiquity, and attempts to estimate the probable influence of Hindu asceticism on the future of India. Dr. Oman's name is, of course, sufficient guarantee of the accuracy and scholarliness of the work and he has succeeded in presenting matter sometimes of considerable difficulty, in so lucid and attractive a form, that the general reader can hardly fail to be interested.

POPULAR HINDUISM. Rs. 1-8.

HINDU RELIGION AND PHILOSOPHY.

THE VEDANTA: Its Theory and Practice. By Swami Saradananda. Anna 1.

THE ARYAN PRAYER BOOK in Sanskrit with an English translation compiled by M. B. Srinivasa Iyengar. Paper bound, As. 4. Linen bound, As. 7, and Silk bound, As. 9.

THE ISA, KENA AND MUNDAKOPANISHADS. Translated by S. Sitarama Sastriar, B.A., with text in Devanagiri and Sankara's commentary. Cloth, Rs. 2. Paper, Rs. 1-8.

THE KATHA AND PRASNOPANISHADS, with the text in Devanagiri and Sankara's commentary, translated by S. Sitarama Sastriar, B.A. Cloth, Rs. 1-8. Paper, Re. 1.

THE AITAREYA AND TAITTIRIYOPANISHAD with the Text in Devanagiri and Sankara's commentary, translated by S. Sitarama Sastriar, B.A., Cloth, Rs. 1-4. Paper, Re. 1.

THE VICISSITUDES OF ARYAN CIVILIZATION IN INDIA. Being an essay which treats of the history of the Vedic and Buddhistic Polities, explaining their origin, prosperity and decline, by M. M. Kunte, B.A. In this book, the strange revolutions through which India has passed during the thousands of years over which her history extends have been reviewed: the principles and conditions of their origin and development have been analysed and the consequences which followed them have been traced with an anxious care which scientific history demands. Reduced Rs. 1-8.

HINDU RELIGION AND PHILOSOPHY.

THE VEDANTA AND ITS RELATION TO MODERN THOUGHT: Being six of a series of Twelve Lectures delivered in Calcutta. By Sitanath Tattvabushan. Paper, Rs. 1-4. Cloth, Rs. 1-8 exclusive of postage.

THE PROBLEM OF EXISTENCE: ITS MYSTERY, STRUGGLE, AND COMFORT IN THE LIGHT OF ARYAN WISDOM. By Manmath C. Malik. *Demy 8vo., cloth.* Rs, 7-14.

Life makes itself manifest in two main features—action and abstraction. Life in continuous action is only observable in the material forces of nature which are incessantly at work without stoppage or rest. Life in abstraction is perceivable in thought alone when the mind withdraws itself wholly from its material associate. There are subordinate divisions as innumerable as the material figures in which life enters for a time, in which the two characteristics are combined in different degrees. To study and to know what life is to solve its mystery, to receive imperishable light, and to secure everlasting and unalloyed happiness.

This book seeks to indicate the method by which the mystery of life may be solved, its delusion dispelled, and individual, national, racial, human advancement towards perfection, if ever attainable on this planet, achieved.

MINOR UPANISHADS, VOL. II. The Vedanta Doctrine of Sankaracharya, comprising (1) Sankara's *Dakshinamurti Stotra* with Sureswara's *Manasollasa*; (2) Sureswara's *Pranava Vartika*; (3) *Dakshinamurti* Upanishad. Cloth, Rs. 1-8. Paper, Rs. 1-4.

HINDU RELIGION AND PHILOSOPHY.

CIVILISATION IN ANCIENT INDIA.—In five Books, *viz.*, (1) The Vedic Age (B. C. 2000 to 1200): (2) The Epic Age (B. C. 1400 to 800); (3) The Age of Laws and Philosophy (B. C. 800 to 300); (4) The Buddhist Age (B C. 300 to A. D. 500) and (5) The Puranic Age (A. D. 500 to the Mahomedan conquest.) Complete in one volume. Rs. 5.

BHAKTI YOGA. By Swami Vivekananda. Re. 1.

KALIDASA : Sakuntala ; or The Lost Ring : an Indian Drama. Translated into English Prose and Verse by Sir Monier Monier-William , K C. I. E. *Seventh Edition.* 282 *pp., cr.* 8 *vo.* Rs. 2-10.

EPICS AND LAYS OF ANCIENT INDIA.—Condensed into English verse, containing the Epics of the Mahabharata and Ramayana, the Hymns of the Rig Veda, Passages from the Upanishads and the Buddhist Literature, the Bridal of Uma and the Penance of Arjuna. Rs. 5.

THE WEB OF INDIAN LIFE.— By Sister Nivedita (Margaret E Noble). Rs. 1-12.

CONTENTS: — 1. The Setting of the Warp ; 2. The Eastern Mother: 3. Of the Hindu Woman as Wife: 4. Love Strong as Death ; 5. The Place of Woman in the National Life ; 6. The Immediate Problems of the Oriental Women ; 7. The Indian Sages ; 8. Noblesse Oblige. A Study of Indian Caste ; 9. The Synthesis of Indian Thought ; 10. The Oriental Experience ; 11. The Wheel of Birth and Death ; 12. The Story of the Great God ; Siva or Mahadev ; 13. The Gospel of the Blessed One ; 14. Islam in India ; 15. An Indian Pilgrimage 16. On the Loom of Time.

Books at Concession Rates

To Subscribers of the Indian Review.

——:o:——

Aspects of the Vedanta.—Essays by various writers. CONTENTS:—The Vedanta in Outline: Pandit Sitanath Tattvabhushan. The Vedanta—Some Reasons for its Study: The late Mr. N. Vythianatha Aiyar, M.A. The Vedanta Religion: Prof. M. Ranga Chariar, M.A. The Ethics of the Vedanta: The late Mr. N. Vythianatha Aiyar, M.A. The Vedanta Doctrine of future Life: Pandit Sitanath Tattvabhushan. The Vedanta: Its Theory and Practice. Swami Saradananda. The Vedanta for the World: Swami Vivekananda: Veda and Vedanta: The late Prof. Max. Müller. The book also contains the opinions of Max. Müller, Dr. Goldstucker, Schopenhauer, Victor Cousin and Dr. P. Deussen ou the Vedanta. The book is dictated to Max Müller and contains an excellent likeness of his. As. 12. To subscribers of the *Indian Review*, As. 8.

Herbert Spencer's Economics.—An exposition by Dr. Guglielmo Salvadori (with a portrait of Herbert Spencer.) Price As. 4. To subscribers of the *Indian Review*, As. 2.

Rudyard Kipling.—A study by John M. Robertson. Author of "Patriotism and Empire" with portraits of Kipling and Robertson. Price As. 2. To subscribers of the *Indian Review*, One Anna.

Industrial India.—By Glyn Barlow, M. A. CONTENTS.—1. Patriotism in Trade. 2. Co-operation. 3. Industrial Exhibitions. 4. The Inquiring Mind. 5. Investigation. 6. Indian Art. 7. Indian Stores. 8. India's Customers. 9. Turning the Corner. 10. Conclusion. Price Rs. 1-8. To subscribers of the *Review*, Re. 1 only.

Shakespeare's Chart of Life.—Being Studies of King Lear, Macbeth, Hamlet and Othello. By Rev. William Miller, LL.D,, C.I.E., *Principal of the Madras Christian College.*

CONTENTS :—1. King Lear and Indian Politics. 2. Macbeth and the Ruin of Souls. 3. Hamlet and the Waste of Life. 4. Othello and the Crash of Character. In his four monographs, Dr. Miller lays constant stress on the fact that the central idea in all Shakespeare's greater dramas is moral. Bound in one vol. Price Rs. 4. To subscribers of the *Indian Review*, Rs. 3. Available for sale separately. Cloth, One Rupee. Wrapper, As. 8.

Report of the Indian Universities' Commission.—Extracts from the Report. Price As. 8. To subscribers of the *Indian Review*, As. 4.

Teaching Universities ; The Senate ; The Syndicate ; Graduates of the Universities ; Governing the College ; Teaching Staff of a College ; Buildings, Furniture, etc. ; Discipline and Residents of students ; Courses of Study ; Classical Languages of the East ; Vernacular Language of India; Matriculation and Government Services; Universities' Funds ; Legislation ; Conclusion. Also Justice Bannerjee's Minute of Dissent in full.

"The Son-in-law abroad" and other Indian Folk-tales of fun-folly, cleverness, cunning, wit and humour. By. P. Ramachandra Row, B.L., *Retired Statutory Civilian.* Price As. 6. To subscribers of the *Indian Review*, As. 4.

Agricultural and Industrial Problems in India,—By Alfred Chatterton, B. SC., *Professor of Engineering, on Special Duty, Madras.*

CONTENTS :—Agricultural:—Water-Lifts, Underground Water-Supply, Well-Irrigation, The Cost of Power, The Value of Wind-Mills in India, Agricultural Education. Industrial :—Tanning in the Madras Presidency, Hand Weaving, Manual Training, Industrial Education, District Board Industrial Schools. Cloth Bound. Price Rs. 2. To subscribers of the *Indian Review*, Re. 1–8.

Ranade and Telang.—Appreciations by the Hon. Mr. G. K. Gokhale, C.I.E., and by Mr. Dinshaw Edulji Wacha, with Portraits of Ranade, Telang, Gokhale and Wacha. Price As. 8. To subscribers of the *Indian Review*, As. 4.

Encyclopædia of Useful Information and Atlas of the World.—By G. W. Ogilvie.

Complete Universal Assistant containing over One Million useful facts, Calculations. Receipts, Processes, Trade Secrets. Rules, Business forms, Legal items, etc. A perfect treasure-house of knowledge on every conceivable subject from the Household to the Manufactory, giving reliable information about everything ; price reduced from Rs. 18–12 to Rs. 8. To subscribers of the *Indian Review*, Rs. 7 only.

"The Son-in-law abroad" and other Indian Folk-tales of fun-folly, cleverness, cunning, wit and humour. By. P. Ramachandra Row, B.L., *Retired Statutory Civilian.* Price As. 6. To subscribers of the *Indian Review*, As. 4.

Agricultural and Industrial Problems in India,—By Alfred Chatterton, B. SC., *Professor of Engineering, on Special Duty, Madras.*

CONTENTS :—Agricultural:—Water-Lifts, Underground Water-Supply, Well-Irrigation, The Cost of Power, The Value of Wind-Mills in India, Agricultural Education. Industrial :—Tanning in the Madras Presidency, Hand Weaving, Manual Training, Industrial Education, District Board Industrial Schools. Cloth Bound. Price Rs. 2. To subscribers of the *Indian Review*, Re. 1–8.

Ranade and Telang.—Appreciations by the Hon. Mr. G. K. Gokhale, C.I.E., and by Mr. Dinshaw Edulji Wacha, with Portraits of Ranade, Telang, Gokhale and Wacha. Price As. 8. To subscribers of the *Indian Review*, As. 4.

Encyclopædia of Useful Information and Atlas of the World.—By G. W. Ogilvie.

Complete Universal Assistant containing over One Million useful facts, Calculations. Receipts, Processes, Trade Secrets. Rules, Business forms, Legal items, etc. A perfect treasure-house of knowledge on every conceivable subject from the Household to the Manufactory, giving reliable information about everything ; price reduced from Rs. 18–12 to Rs. 8. To subscribers of the *Indian Review*, Rs. 7 only.

The Durbar Album.—Published by Wiele and Klien, *Photographers.*

A Permanent Photographic Record of the chief events which took place during the Coronation Durbar containing Portraits of the chief personages who took a leading part in the same. The book contains over 120 different views executed in the best style of photographic engraving, Portraits of Their Majesties, the King Emperor and the Queen, His Excellency the Viceroy, the Governors of Madras, Bombay, and other Provinces, and Lord Kitchener, the Ruling Princes and Nobles in full Durbar Custom, &c., &c. Price Rs. Ten. To subscribers of the *Indian Review*, Rs. 8–8.

Maitreyi.—A Vedic Story in six chapters, by Pandit Sitanath Tattvabhushan. Pric As. 8. To subscribers of the *Indian Review*, As. 4.

1500 Tit-Bits of Indian Law being a collection of the general principles of Law, Criminal and Civil, in force throughout India, for the use of students and non-legal public with full Index by a Lawyer. Price Rs. 5. To subscribers of " the *Indian Review*, Rs. 4–8.

King Lear and Indian Politics.—By the Hon. Rev. William Miller, C.I.E., LL.D., Principal of the Madras Christian College.

After preliminary remarks on the date and sources of the play, Dr. Miller sets himself to determine the point of view from which it ought to be regarded as a whole. He finds two great thoughts running through the tragedy, and traces, at considerable length, how these find expression in the history of each of the principal personages. He goes on to show how the thoughts thus translated into action on the stage cast light on the chief problems of human life, and especially on the right constitution and healthy growth of human society. The book closes with a discussion of the way in which the principles exemplified in King Lear bear on the present state and future progress of social and political life in India. Cloth bound One Rupee. In wrapper As. 8.

Uniform with this volume and sold at the same price :—(1) Othello and the Crash of Character. (2) Hamlet and the Waste of Life. (3) Macbeth and the Ruin of Souls. These four monographs are bound together in one volume under the title "Shakespeare's Chart of Life." Rs. 4. To subscribers of the *Indian Review*, Rs. 3.

Macbeth and the Ruin of Souls-—By the Hon. Rev. William Miller, C.I.E., LL.D., Principal of the Madras Christian College.

The book starts with a discussion of the materials on which the tragedy is based. It regards the history of Macbeth as being in the main a study of how evil when once yielded to gradually induces total moral ruin. It shows how the central " business of the play is to mark the steps by which, and the influences under which, a man who at first appears worthy of admiration becomes all that a man ought not to be." After tracing the moral ruin of Macbeth, it shows how by a different process Lady Macbeth arrives at an equally lamentable end. It then discusses each of the other characters in sufficient detail to show how the assaults of evil upon each of them are baffled on the one hand or are successful on the the other. The book arrives at the conclusion that it is " as a supreme example of the strife which rages endlessly and everywhere on earth between the kingdom of heaven and the kingdom of hell that *Macbeth* holds the place of the most solemnly instructive of the gifts of literature to the generations of weak humanity." Cloth Bound, Re. One. In wrappers, As. 8.

Uniform with this volume and sold at the same price:—(1) Othello and the Crash of Character. (2) Hamlet and the Waste of Life. (3) King Lear and Indian Politics. These four monographs are bound together in one volume under the title " Shakespeare's Chart of Life. Rs. 4. To subscribers of the *Indian Review*, Rs. 3.

Hamlet and the Waste of Life.—By the Hon. Rev. William Miller, C.I.E., LL.D., Principal of the Madras Christian College.

In this new criticism of a much criticized play, Dr. Miller after some introductory observation, re-states his views as to the central idea in all Shakespeare's greater dramas being moral, and as to the moral benefit which ought to accrue to one who studies them with care. In this light he examined the character of Hamlet and discusses some of the warmly debated questions which cannot be avoided by one who tries to understand it.

After treating of the characters of the subordinate personages in the play, especially of those who serve as foils to Hamlet, Dr. Miller draws a comparison between the Prince of Denmark and Indian students, of whom he says that "if they have something of Hamlet's strength, they have lamentably much of Hamlet's weakness." He closes with a brief statement of the main lesson which Young India may learn from the drama most widely known of all the works of Shakespeare. Cloth Bound, Re. One. In wrappers, As. 8.

Uniform with this volume and sold at the same price.—(1) Othello and the Crash of Character. (2) Macbeth and the Ruin of Souls. (3) King Lear and Indian Politics. These four monographs are bound together in one volume under the title "Shakespeare's Chart of Life." Rs. 4. To subscribers of the *Indian Review*, Rs. 3.

Othello and the Crash of Character.—By the Hon. Rev. William Miller, C.I.E., LL.D., Principal of the Madras Christian College.

In this monograph, as in his earlier Studies of *King Lear*, *Macbeth* and *Hamlet*, Dr. Miller directs attention mainly to the moral truths illustrated in the drama, maintaining these to be its proper centre from the artistic as well as the practical point of view. In delineating Othello and Desdemona, he points out that, along with much that was good and noble, there were defects and faults in both which opened the way for all the calamities that came on them * * * Iago he regards as the willing instrument of those evil powers which are always ready to take advantage of the openings which the want of watchful care on the part even of the best too often yield. Dr. Miller looks upon "Othello" as a revelation of forces which "more or less strongly affect the inner life of every man" and maintains that the way in which those forces are disentangled in it "from all that is accidental or superficial will be held by those who read wisely to be full compensation for the pain which the study of so unrelieved a tragedy must cause." Cloth Bound, Re. One. In wrappers, As. 8.

Uniform with this volume and sold at the same price:—(1) Hamlet and the Waste of Life. (2) Macbeth and the Ruin of Souls. (3) King Lear and Indian Politics. These four monographs are bound together in one volume under the title "Shakespeare's Chart of Life." Rs. 4. To subscribers of the *Indian Review*, Rs. 3.

G.A. NATESAN & Co., ESPLANADE, MADRAS.